THE
JOHNSTOWN FLOOD
OF 1889

GREAT HISTORIC DISASTERS

GREAT HISTORIC DISASTERS

THE JOHNSTOWN FLOOD OF 1889

RACHEL A. KOESTLER-GRACK

CHELSEA HOUSE
PUBLISHERS
An imprint of Infobase Publishing

THE JOHNSTOWN FLOOD OF 1889

Chelsea House
An imprint of Infobase Publishing
132 West 31st Street
New York NY 10001

Library of Congress Cataloging-in-Publication Data
Koestler-Grack, Rachel A., 1973-
Johnstown flood of 1889 / Rachel A. Koestler-Grack.
  p. cm.—(Great historic disasters)
Includes bibliographical references and index.
ISBN: 978-0-7910-9763-2 (hardcover)
1. Floods—Pennsylvania—Johnstown (Cambria County)—History—19th century—Juvenile literature. 2. Johnstown (Cambria County, Pa.)—History—19th century—Juvenile literature. I. Title. II. Series.
F159.J7K64 2008
974.8'77—dc22   2008004894

Chelsea House books are available at special discounts when purchased in bulk quantities for businesses, associations, institutions, or sales promotions. Please call our Special Sales Department in New York at (212) 967-8800 or (800) 322-8755.

You can find Chelsea House on the World Wide Web at http://www.chelseahouse.com

Text design by Annie O'Donnell
Cover design by Ben Peterson

Printed in the United States of America

Bang KT 10 9 8 7 6 5 4 3 2 1

This book is printed on acid-free paper.

All links and Web addresses were checked and verified to be correct at the time of publication. Because of the dynamic nature of the Web, some addresses and links may have changed since publication and may no longer be valid.

Contents

Introduction:
Ten Minutes of Terror

On Friday, May 31, 1889, the water in front of the Heiser dry-goods store on Washington Street had been knee-deep all afternoon. Never, in all the years of floods at Johnstown, had the water crept so far into that part of town. That morning, people had been in and out of the store, buying supplies to get them through the thick of spring flooding. The floor was slick with mud, and the scent of tobacco and wet wool hung in the warm, damp air. George Heiser was much too busy taking care of customers to pay attention to what was happening outside. But by early afternoon, the street had sunk under two feet of water. The local shops were all but empty, except for an occasional customer.

Shortly before 4:00, George Heiser sent his 16-year-old son, Victor, out to the barn to check on the horses. Earlier, they had tied the animals to their stalls. George worried that if the water got much higher, the horses might strangle themselves. So, Victor went out to untie them. The new glossy red barn stood on higher ground at the back of their lot. Victor slipped off his shoes and socks and pulled on a pair of shorts. Then, he waded across the yard through the hammering rain. Within a few minutes, he had untied the horses and was on his way out the door. At that moment, he heard an awful noise.

Terrified, he froze in the doorway, barely able to breathe. The roar in the distance grew louder and louder. Every few seconds, he heard an enormous crash that shook the valley. Across the yard in the second-story window, he noticed his father waving at him to get back into the barn and upstairs. A couple of weeks earlier, George had cut a trapdoor through the barn roof, just in case of trouble. Quickly, Victor raced up the stairs, went through the trapdoor, and climbed onto the roof.

Once on the roof, he peered out across the top of his house. No more than two blocks away, he saw what was causing all the racket. It looked to him like a tremendous wall of wreckage, dark and spinning with rooftops, timber, and planks. Believing it was his final moment on Earth, he pulled out his pocket watch and looked at the time. He wondered how long it would take for him to pass from this world to the next. When the massive wave struck Washington Street, Victor watched his home crushed like an eggshell. At the same moment, the barn was ripped from its footings and started rolling like a barrel. Hand over hand and foot over foot, he clawed at tin and wood. He ran and stumbled and crawled and somehow managed to stay on top of the twirling barn. In front of him, he saw the house of their neighbor. The barn was speeding straight for it.

At the exact moment of impact, Victor jumped onto the roof of the house just as the walls crumbled and the roof started plunging downward. He scaled the steep pitch of the roof, struggling to keep his balance. Still, he saw no water around him. The deafening noise was overwhelming. On every side, wreckage was cracking, twisting, and splitting. Broken glass and planks shot through the air. Victor felt as if he were in the middle of a huge explosion.

The roof that he was riding started to sink, so he caught another house that had rammed into one side. He grabbed onto the eaves of the passing roof, clinging to the boards, his feet dangling below him. Over and over, he tried to get a foothold on the roof but failed. His fingernails dug into the spongy shingles. If he let go, he knew he would drown. For years afterward, he had many nightmares about those speeding seconds when his life almost ended. Finally, he could hold on no longer. He fell backward, down through the wet, dusty mist, until he slammed onto a section of red roof from his new barn.

Now, for the first time, Victor saw the water. He was riding the tidal wave, flat on his stomach and hanging on with every bit of strength left in him. Ahead of him and below, the wave devoured Johnstown. Most of what Victor saw sailing by him that afternoon later melted into a gray, hideous blur. But one spilt-second glimpse would be branded in his memory forever.

The entire Mussante family rode past him, kneeling on a barn floor. Mr. Mussante, an Italian with a draping mustache, was a fruit dealer on Washington Street. He had a wife and two children. Victor knew them well. As they sped by him, they were busy throwing items into a Saratoga trunk. Seconds later, a mound of wreckage rose out of the water and crushed them.

Victor, however, had no time to think about what had just happened to his neighbors. He was headed into a mound of rubbish lodged between the Methodist Church and a three-story brick building on the other side of a now-buried Locust Street. The next thing Victor knew, he was among the wreckage, dodging falling beams. Suddenly, a freight car sailed over his head. At the time, it looked like the most colossal thing he had ever seen. He knew it would be impossible to jump far enough out of the way. But just before it crashed down on top of him, the brick building collapsed. His raft, as he later described it, "shot out from beneath the freight car like a bullet from a gun."

He found himself rushing down the open water. Although he was still riding the rapid current, he was in far less danger. He took a moment to look around him. People were struggling and drowning on all sides. From time to time, he would recognize a face. Then, in a flash, they would disappear beneath the flood.

The Johnstown Flood of 1889 resulted from a series of human errors and an unusually rainy season. An entire city virtually washed away as a torrent of water broke through the local dam, leaving behind the remains of destroyed homes and businesses. More than 2,000 people were killed in the tragedy.

Victor's raft was moving toward Stony Creek. He had his eyes fixed on the mountainside, which looked almost close enough to touch by now. Just beyond the mountain was the stone bridge. Both places could be possible landings for him. But then, all of a sudden, he got caught in the backcurrent. It thrust him toward the town of Kernville.

Up ahead, he could see a two-story building that had held firm to its foundation. His speed slowed down, and he was able to hop up onto the roof where a small group of people were already stranded. Safe on the rooftop, Victor pulled out his fancy silver watch to check the time. Having made it through the wave, he figured he might be in this world a while longer after all. For a moment, he studied the intricate etching on the cover. The watch had been a birthday present from his father. When he popped it open, he was amazed to see that it still worked. Even more astonishing, though, was the time it read. Everything that had just happened to him—his home destroyed, his neighbors killed—had taken place in just 10 terrifying minutes.

GREAT FLOOD

The Johnstown Flood of 1889 is one of the nation's worst "natural" disasters. Within 10 minutes, a raging wall of water and debris, 35 to 40 feet tall and rushing at 40 miles per hour, washed away the entire center of the city, killing thousands. After years of finding bodies buried deep in the mud, it was determined that an estimated 2,209 people died in Johnstown on May 31. Of these victims, 396 were children ages 10 or younger. Ninety-eight children were orphaned, and 99 entire families were wiped out.

For years, trouble had loomed at the South Fork Dam, just 14 miles up the Conemaugh River. The dam had been neglected and mismanaged. It was only a saturated spring and heavy downpour away from bursting. The nightmare became a reality in 1889.

Floods are devastating monsters. At eight pounds per gallon, rushing water has tremendous force. It can carry off almost anything. The amount of water unleashed into the Conemaugh Valley when the South Fork dam broke on May 31, 1889, was about 20 million gallons. Like a snowball rolling down a powdery hill, the tumbling flood added mass as it ripped away 14 miles of timber, telegraph poles, houses, boulders, and freight cars. The city of Johnstown, Pennsylvania, became etched in history on that fateful day. After the torrent passed through, 27,000 people were left homeless and stunned. The damage done to property topped $30 million.

In the days that followed, survivors picked through moldering heaps of ruins, desperately searching for loved ones or just some fragment of their lives. Some people, pinned in the debris, were rescued. Others lay lifeless in the twisted rubble. The dead were lined up by the hundreds in morgues throughout the city and in towns farther down the Conemaugh River. Pine coffins, stacked three deep, mounded every scrap of dry land.

The full drama and exact details of the Johnstown Flood will never be told. Much of the story disappeared in the yellow-brown waters with those who died, their voices forever muted. But from the survivors, historians pieced together a jagged yet horrifying account of the events that unfolded on Memorial Day 1889. Their stories are frightening and heartrending. Out of their tragedy, however, an amazing spirit of survival arose. The people of Johnstown picked themselves up out of devastation and somehow rebuilt their lives. Their story is a testament of courage and determination.

Booming Steel Town

Johnstown, Pennsylvania, is nestled deep in the Allegheny Mountains near the Conemaugh River. The area was first settled in the 1790s by a Swiss immigrant named Joseph Schantz, more commonly called Joseph Johns. Together with his wife and four children, Johns began building a settlement he named Conemaugh, after the neighboring mountain river. As the years passed, more settlers trickled into "Johns' town." Later, Conemaugh was renamed Johnstown, in honor of the man who founded it.

As Pennsylvania's transportation system grew, Johnstown became an important town along the Main Line Canal. The Main Line was a combination of railroad tracks and canal passages that carried both people and supplies across Pennsylvania. Before long, the Cambria Iron Company moved into Johnstown. The Conemaugh Valley offered the natural resources for making both iron and steel. Johnstown quickly boomed into a leading iron- and steel-producing center. With plenty of jobs available at Cambria Iron Company, the city thundered to life. By 1889, the population had climbed to a staggering 30,000 residents.

Johnstown had been built on a nearly level floodplain, where the Conemaugh River and the Stony Creek meet. For the men who worked 12-hour days, 6 days a week, surrounded by molten metal, Johnstown was like a smoldering pit, framed by dense forest ridges called "hogbacks." On the hillsides close to the mills, the sickly fingers of trees were charred and leafless. The Cambria Iron Company kept its giant three-ton converters running day and night making steel for rails, barbed wire, plowshares, and railroad track bolts. Coughing up plumes of smoke, the city clanked and whistled and rumbled loud enough to be heard miles away.

In 1889, Johnstown was not a pretty place. However, the countryside that hugged it was magnificent. From Main Street, a visitor could look off in every direction and marvel at the rolling waves of green gently riding the mountainside. The view brought to mind that, somewhere beyond the noisy clamoring of Johnstown, a peaceful world existed.

SAILBOATS IN THE MOUNTAINS

That place was just 14 miles up the Conemaugh River at a resort called the South Fork Fishing and Hunting Club. There, 61 elite club members visited secluded cottages on weekends and throughout the summer. From their deep porches, members enjoyed the stunning view of Lake Conemaugh, a man-made mountain lake. Constructed in 1853, Lake Conemaugh once served as a feeder for Pennsylvania's Main Line Canal system. One of the nuisances of the canal system was that the mountain water levels fluctuated with the seasons. Those in charge of canal transportation felt they could better deal with the unpredictable water levels if they built a dam. Over the years, the reservoir created by the dam had been called by many names. Originally, it was known as the Western Reservoir. Close to the town of South Fork, however, locals referred to the reservoir as the South Fork Dam. At various other points in history and with numerous owners, the dam was called the Old Reservoir, the Three Mile Dam, and finally Lake Conemaugh by members of the South Fork Fishing and

Hunting Club. Fed by six streams, Lake Conemaugh was one of the largest man-made bodies of water in the United States. When full, the reservoir held 3.6 million gallons, about 20 tons of water.

When building the dam, workers packed and pounded layers of clay and rock. Each layer was two feet thick. Workers skimmed every layer with water and let it sit for a while to make it watertight before starting the next layer. This technique is called "puddling." Puddled layers helped the earth settle into place, making the dam much stronger than if it were just a heap of stone and clay. Behind the clay and earth section were a core of broken slate, shale, and other small rocks mixed with

Built to hold back the waters of Lake Conemaugh, the South Fork Dam was improperly adjusted and badly maintained by the owners of the South Fork Hunting and Fishing Club. Before the flood, the lake was about 3 miles long, 1 mile wide, and 60 feet deep; after the flood, however, the lake and dam disappeared *(above)*.

dirt for extra weight and added strength. The interior of the dam was covered with a skin of small stones to protect the clay. This layer is known as a "riprap." Another riprap covered the exterior, or downstream side, of the dam. This layer was made up of massive boulders, some weighing more than 10 tons.

Five cast-iron pipes, each two feet in diameter, lay across the base of the dam. The pipes ran through a stone culvert and were fitted with valves that could be opened and closed from a wooden control tower. These pipes were vital for the dam's security and safety because they controlled the level of water in the lake. During times of high water, the excess could be drained through the base of the dam, reducing the risk of overflow. Also, the pipes provided a way to drain the reservoir in case the dam needed to be repaired.

Along the eastern end, there was also a 70-foot-wide spill-way. At the time of construction, the spillway ran about 10 feet below the top of the dam. It was cut into the natural rocky hillside as a second safety precaution. The excess water would run out of the spillway before it could overtop the dam.

By the end of a 17-year construction, the massive dam stretched 931 feet, with a stocky 270-foot-thick base. It was 72 feet high and 10 feet wide at the top. Depending on the level of water in the reservoir, the surface area of the lake ranged between 400 and 450 acres. When the dam was full, the distance around the lake was roughly seven miles. Although unmistakably impressive, the dam unnerved many people, who feared it would give way one day. Perched high above the valley, the lake waters had no place to go but downstream. A break would wipe out all the towns between South Fork and Johnstown. To some locals, the Western Reservoir was a disaster waiting to happen.

For the first 10 years, though, the dam held steady. The level of the lake was kept well below capacity, which helped keep the pressure down. In July 1862, however, a section of the dam near the center, maybe as much as 200 feet wide, washed out. Apparently, a portion of the stone culvert that held the sluice pipes had collapsed, which in turn caused the washout. At first, news of the dam breaking caused a flare of fright. Luckily, though, the lake level was low at the time, and the valley below was in the dry season. The minimal flooding caused no serious damage to the valley towns. At the dam, workers opened the pipe valves to reduce the pressure and to keep the dam from completely collapsing. Relief and calm swept through the valley. Many townsfolk began to rethink their worries about the dam. Perhaps a break would not be as catastrophic as they had first thought.

In 1875, the Pennsylvania Railroad sold the South Fork Dam and surrounding area to Congressman John Reilly. Some historians believe it was Reilly who removed the five sluice pipes from the damaged stone culvert and then sold them as scrap. His poor decision compromised the safety of the dam. Without the sluice pipes, water could not be drained from the lake to reduce pressure or to make repairs on the dam. However, it was not Reilly's problem for long. In 1879, he sold the land around the South Fork Dam to Benjamin Ruff, a railroad tunnel contractor from Pittsburgh.

Ruff saw grand potential in the area. The industrial era of the late 1800s was transforming the nation. Many cities were plagued by soot- and smoke-filled air. In some industrial towns, the atmosphere was so blanketed with smoke that the Sun's rays were partially blocked. People would jump at the chance to have a cottage in the mountains, just a short train ride from the hazy, steel-grinding Pennsylvania cities. Ruff decided to open the South Fork Fishing and Hunting Club, set beside a beautiful lake in the crisp, clean mountain air.

His first task, however, would be repairs. Little had been done to fix South Fork Dam after it had broken in 1862, except to lower the water level. Without the body of water that the dam was originally designed to hold, the club would have nothing more to offer members than other popular mountain retreats

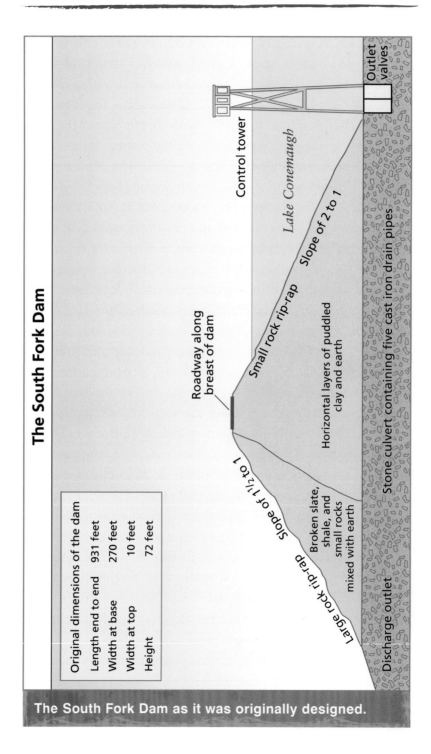

The South Fork Dam

Original dimensions of the dam	
Length end to end	931 feet
Width at base	270 feet
Width at top	10 feet
Height	72 feet

Control tower

Lake Conemaugh

Roadway along breast of dam

Small rock rip-rap

Slope of 2 to 1

Horizontal layers of puddled clay and earth

Slope of 1½ to 1

Large rock rip-rap

Broken slate, shale, and small rocks mixed with earth

Stone culvert containing five cast iron drain pipes

Outlet valves

Discharge outlet

The South Fork Dam as it was originally designed.

of the time. Lake Conemaugh would have to be the center of the resort, enticing members with boating, fishing, and swimming. All of these activities required a large lake, not one the shrunken size of the reservoir in 1879. The 200-foot damaged section would have to be mended. The gouge spanned about 20 percent of the dam's total length. Therefore, repairing the damage was no small feat.

Repair work was not done under the professional and watchful eye of an engineer, though. Ruff had hired an engineer from Pittsburgh, but his on-site input was limited. Workers failed to puddle the area being repaired, as had been done in the original construction. Instead of replacing the sluice pipes, the openings were merely filled. Holes and leaks were patched with whatever material Ruff could find—hay, branches, even manure.

Ruff wanted Lake Conemaugh to astound his members in every way possible. The most stunning view of the lake was from the carriage road that stretched across the top of the dam. Most club members would travel by train to South Fork. From there, they would take a chauffeured carriage to the clubhouse or to a private cottage. The sight they would lay eyes on would be that of Lake Conemaugh from the carriage road atop the dam. However, the road was as narrow as 10 feet in places—not enough room for carriages or wagons to pass each other. Although a large lake was critical, Ruff decided Lake Conemaugh did not need to be quite as big as the reservoir could be. His original plan was to lower both the height of the dam and the spillway in order to widen the carriage road. However, Ruff quickly discovered that without proper equipment, cutting down the solid rock of the spillway was nearly impossible. He went ahead with his plans to widen the carriage road and skimmed two to three feet off the dam. By lowering the dam, the carriage road was widened to at least 20 feet; it was 30 feet wide in some spots.

Ruff's decision to lower the dam was seriously flawed, though. Without chiseling down the spillway an equal amount, the spillway would not be nearly as effective in preventing the water from overtopping the dam. Just before opening the club, Ruff paid an expensive $750 to stock Lake Conemaugh with black bass. Naturally, he did not want his investment to escape out the spillway. So, he placed a weir across the spillway. The weir's metal screens allowed water, but not fish, to pass through. The screens had to be cleaned out from time to time because they became clogged with leaves, twigs, and other debris.

By the spring of 1881, Lake Conemaugh was filling up, and the dam was holding water. The South Fork Fishing and Hunting Club was ready to welcome its members. The wealthy elite from Pittsburgh and other eastern cities retreated to the club for fishing or sailing. Many people commented on the bizarre sight of sailboats floating in the mountains. In the beginning, the South Fork Fishing and Hunting Club seemed to be a marvelous concept. Quickly, some of the country's most prestigious businessmen wanted a share of the club, including wealthy industrialist Andrew Carnegie.

2 The Storm Begins

On the morning of May 30, 1889, a glittering frost twinkled in the valley below South Fork Dam. This Memorial Day began like any other in Johnstown. As the morning ticked by, plenty of visitors emerged and crowded the streets. Some came for the parade while others were in town for a convention.

A light rain began at four in the afternoon. By this time, though, most of the holiday crowds were back from the cemetery. Not much more than a cool mist, the rain came down in fine, soft sheets. Still, the townspeople grumbled. There had been more than a hundred days of rain that year. The rivers were already too high. Of course, the rivers and streams swelled every spring. Some years they pushed their banks and filled the lower half of town to the top doorstep.

Floods had become a sign of the season, like dogwood blooming on the mountain. However, the rivers had gotten increasingly restless in recent years. The first flood recorded in Johnstown was in 1808, when waters destroyed a small dam that stretched across the Stony Creek. About 12 years later, the Pumpkin Floods in the fall swept hundreds of pumpkins from Cambria County into town. In 1847, another little dam on the

Stony Creek gave way. Five years later, in 1880, a dam built by Cambria Iron as a feeder for the mills burst. In 1885, the Stony Creek dam broke again, and it did so practically every year after until 1889.

There were logical reasons for the flooding problems in Johnstown. The city had been growing and needed more lumber and more space. Load after load of timber was stripped off the mountains and nearby hills. In Johnstown, workers narrowed river channels to make room for new buildings or to build bridges. The forests retained huge amounts of water in the soil, about 800 tons per acre. In mountain country, the trees held the soil in the summer and the snow in the winter. Without forestland, spring thaws and summer thunderstorms sent torrents racing down the mountainside. Each year, the rushing water grew worse as soil and ground cover washed away. In the valley, the water slid into steadily shrinking rivers. The thin rivers could not handle the increased runoff, and flash floods became common. Some Johnstown people figured the narrowing riverbanks would simply force the water to dig deeper channels. The riverbeds were nearly all rock, however. With nowhere to go, the rivers rose, and quickly—sometimes as much as two to three feet in an hour.

Except in spring, the rivers behaved themselves for the rest of the year. The Little Conemaugh and the Stony Creek were more like rocky, oversize mountain streams than rivers. Each one was about 60 to 80 yards wide. Normally, they had a swift current, and in spring, they ran wild. But by August, there were places on either river that someone could jump across on dry stones. The Little Conemaugh, much swifter than Stony, rushes in from the Allegheny Mountains in the east. It began near the top of the mountain, about 18 miles from Johnstown, at the coal town of Lilly. From there, an elevation of 2,300 feet, the river dropped 1,147 feet to Johnstown. Stony Creek flowed from the south. Broader and deeper, it was fed by smaller streams, such as Beaver Dam Run, Fallen Timber Run, and Shade Creek.

At Johnstown, the two rivers joined to form the Conemaugh. Farther west, this river joined the Loyalhanna to form the Kiskiminetas, which flowed into the Allegheny near Pittsburgh.

The spring of 1889 was unusually wet in the Conemaugh Valley. Heavy snowfalls in the late winter and early spring had saturated the ground. The valley experienced heavy rainfall

Established at the fork of the Little Conemaugh and Stony Creek Rivers, Johnstown was already prone to flooding during a normal rainy season. As the town grew, people settled closer to the banks of the rivers and even began to narrow some of the riverbed to create more space for real estate. When the dam broke and Lake Conemaugh was released, Johnstown was directly in the path of the rushing water.

in April and May. People were tired of the dreary weather but seemed to shrug it off. Although there had been reports of a massive storm system only miles away, they were unaware how dangerous more heavy rains could become.

After giving the town a fresh rinse, the rain stopped at about five that evening. As night settled in, streetlights dotted Main, where rolls of laughter spilled out of saloon windows. Much progress had been made in this area, especially for a town buried deep in the mountains. There was a new railroad station and hospital. A telephone exchange had started service that year, and already, 70 phones were working throughout town. Quite a few houses had bathrooms. The Hubert House, a new hotel, had an elevator and steam heat. A street railway stretched out to Woodvale and another up to Moxham. Almost every home had electricity and natural gas. Typewriters sat on the desktops of most offices, and several people in town had bought one of the new Kodak "detective" cameras.

Meanwhile, at the South Fork Fishing and Hunting Club, the wind had picked up by late afternoon. Gusts whipped down from the mountains, flattening tall grasses along the lakeshore and kicking up whitecaps across the lake.

Sometime after dark, as storm clouds rolled in, the club's resident engineer, John Parke, Jr., stepped out onto the long front porch of the clubhouse. He leaned over the railing and tipped his face up to the blackening sky. Unable to see much in the dark, he stepped down the porch stairs and walked down the trail that led through the trees to the club cottages. He noticed that, although the wind was still sharp and blustery, the sky had started to clear. This sight puzzled him. On the mountain, windstorms almost always meant a heavy downpour was fast approaching. The local men called the winds "thunder-gusts." In these storms, the storm clouds would seem to suffocate the landscape and rain would drum down relentlessly. Wild flashes of blue-white lightning would crack the coal-colored sky, and rumbles of thunder would rattle every window along the lakeshore. Then, as suddenly as it had arrived, the storm would lift back into the sky.

On this night, it seemed to Parke, there would be no storm. He headed back to the clubhouse and, around 9:30, went upstairs to bed. Around 11:00, an angry rain began pounding on the roof, heavy sheets slamming against the clubhouse. And all down the valley, for miles and miles, trees heaved and tossed in a ferocious wind. Apparently, the storm had started in Kansas and Nebraska two days earlier, on May 28. The following day, hard rains swept through Kansas, Missouri, Illinois, Michigan, Indiana, Kentucky, and Tennessee. Trains were delayed, roads were washed out. In Kansas, tornado-force winds had flattened a dozen farms, killing several people. Warnings had been telegraphed east, alerting the Middle Atlantic states to be prepared for severe storms. But nothing could have prepared Pennsylvania for what was coming next.

RISING WATERS

By morning on Friday, May 31, Stony Creek and the Little Conemaugh were rising at a rate of 18 to 24 inches per hour. Slowly, Johnstown streets sank into the murky, yellow-brown floodwater. From one end of town to the other, the waters ranged from 2 to 10 feet deep. The flood was already deeper than the one in 1887, making it Johnstown's worst flood on record. For a while, the rain eased, replaced by a thick mist that shadowed the valley. A dark sky threatened another downpour, though. Workmen at the Cambria mills had been sent home to take care of their families. While townsfolk grumbled about the water in their cellars, children splashed in the streets, floating boxes and boards around like boats. All along Main Street, shopkeepers scurried to move their goods to upper levels. As the morning slugged along, the tireless rains returned. Around 11:00, a log boom burst up the Stony Creek and released an avalanche of logs that stampeded through the valley until they jammed between the massive arches of the stone bridge.

About the same time, the Stony Creek ripped down the Poplar Street Bridge. Then, floodwaters swept away the Cambria City Bridge. At St. John's Catholic Church—far uptown and

Johnstown Floods of 1936 and 1977

The Johnstown flood of 1889 was the most devastating flood ever experienced in the country. Until September 11, 2001, it stood in U.S. history as the event where the greatest number of people died in a disaster in a single day. However, it was not the last flood to hit Johnstown.

On March 17, 1936, Johnstown suffered another devastating flood caused by heavy runoff of melting snow and three days of rain. Before the flood receded the next day, water reached 14 feet in some places. Two dozen people died, and 77 buildings were destroyed. Another 3,000 buildings were severely damaged. Altogether, there was $41 million in property damages.

The federal government immediately went to work to help rehabilitate Johnstown. The Works Progress Administration (WPA) mustered every able-bodied man in a four-county diameter to provide assistance. Seven thousand men showed up to dig out the town. Still, Johnstown pleaded with Washington for more help. The White House was swamped with 15,000 letters from locals. President Franklin D. Roosevelt responded by visiting Johnstown. After seeing the disaster for himself, he authorized the U.S. Army Corps of Engineers to build channels in the rivers that flowed through town. The $8.7 million project was called the Local Flood Protection Program, aimed to increase the water capacity of rivers and prevent future floods.

supposedly beyond the reach of the spring floods—a funeral had to be postponed midway through the service because the waters were so deep. The rains needled almost every city in the

According to the Local Flood Protection Program, the channels were supposed to keep Johnstown "flood-free." But on July 20, 1977, a line of severe thunderstorms stalled over the Conemaugh Valley. As much as a foot of rain fell in some areas. Small streams—such as Salmon's Run, Sam's Run, and Peggy's Run—carved new courses and plowed through highways, apartment buildings, business, and homes.

At Laurel Run Reservoir, an earthen water-supply dam broke, one of several to fail that day. In Johnstown, waters overflowed the channel system. The U.S. Army Corps of Engineers claimed the water level could have risen 11 feet higher if the channel system had never been built.

Once again, state and federal governments and nonprofit agencies such as the Red Cross and the Salvation Army stepped in to help. On July 21, President Jimmy Carter declared some badly hit counties disaster areas, including Cambria. As in 1936, the U.S. Army Corps of Engineers was willing to lend a hand in cleanup efforts. By the end of the ordeal, 85 people had died, and property damages had scaled to $300 million. Hundreds of people were homeless, finding shelter in churches; schools; fire halls; and the dormitories of the University of Pennsylvania, Johnstown; and, later, in special trailer parks. Over the following year, the federal government spent $200 million rebuilding demolished public facilities. For the past 30 years, Johnstown has escaped major flooding. Perhaps some people wonder if time is running out before another one hits.

valley with inconveniences. Bear Run had risen six feet and washed out a quarter mile of railroad track. Trains were held up in South Fork and East Conemaugh awaiting orders from the Pennsylvania Railroad.

For a few locals, the flood revived old fears about South Fork Dam. They grabbed what belongings they could carry and moved to higher ground. As they waded through the streets, carrying bundles of clothing over their heads, some heard a few snickers from other townsfolk who thought they were being too timid. For the rest of Johnstown, townspeople were willing to wait out what appeared to be just another dreary spring flood.

Fourteen miles up the twisting waters of the Little Conemaugh, a more anxious attitude was growing. At 6:30 that morning, John Parke awoke and peered out the window in his clubhouse bedroom. The hammering rain had lessened, and he could barely see through the gray haze that had dropped over the trees and lake. When he stepped out on the front porch, he heard a monstrous roar like a waterfall coming from the head of the lake to the south. He noticed that the lake had risen two feet overnight and now churned just two to three feet below the crest of the dam. From the clubhouse, Parke could not determine, though, how much and how fast the six streams were feeding the lake. He and another club workman set out in a rowboat to take a look at the incoming creeks.

As they rowed against the strong current, they realized that they were floating on top of a four-strand barbed-wire fence that usually stood a good distance back from the shoreline. They continued to row across another hundred yards or more of what was normally a cow pasture. Finally, they came to the place where South Fork Creek emptied into the lake. The creek had swelled into a wicked torrent and strayed from its natural path, sweeping through the woods and stripping branches, bark, and leaves from the trees five feet up the trunks. The two men pulled their boat onto what seemed like the driest piece of land in sight and headed up the creek on foot. In every direction, the

As the floodwaters rose, some began to leave town with their belongings, nervously eyeing the dam as they fled to higher ground. Others who resided near the dam *(above)* were apprehensive, as well, because they could see and hear water from nearby creeks rushing into the reservoir, increasing the pressure on the South Fork Dam.

woods churned with water. When they returned to the boat, the water had risen enough in that short time to set it slightly adrift. From what he had seen, Parke figured the water was rising an inch every 10 minutes. At that rate, it was only a matter of time before Lake Conemaugh would spill over the top of the South Fork Dam.

Back at the club, a crowd of about 50 locals from South Fork huddled under a cluster of trees, watching events unfold at the dam. While Parke was out inspecting the streams, Colonel Elias Unger, the president and manager of the South Fork Fishing and Hunting Club, was desperately trying to save the dam. Benjamin Ruff had passed away two years before. Earlier that morning, Unger had slipped on his coat and boots

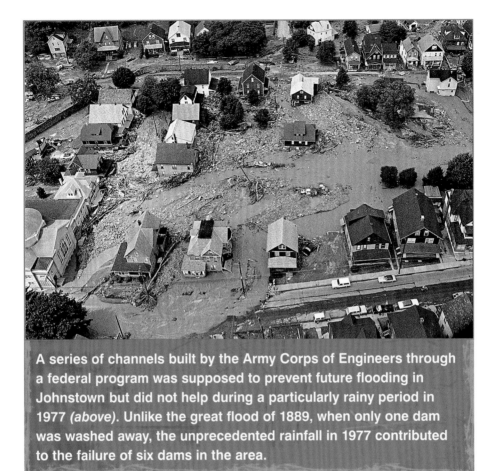

A series of channels built by the Army Corps of Engineers through a federal program was supposed to prevent future flooding in Johnstown but did not help during a particularly rainy period in 1977 *(above)*. Unlike the great flood of 1889, when only one dam was washed away, the unprecedented rainfall in 1977 contributed to the failure of six dams in the area.

and walked down the hill to a sturdy wooden bridge that spanned the spillway. From there, it looked as if the entire valley was submerged in water. Unger took some measurements of the rising water and at that moment decided to call in a work crew to strengthen the dam. Unger understood the possible danger to Conemaugh Valley if the dam burst and let go of all the water at once. Undoubtedly, he was also aware of his responsibility to the club and its members. Without the dam, there was no lake. Without Lake Conemaugh, the club was simply a collection of cottages, a clubhouse, a few outbuildings, and a handful of useless boats.

By the time Parke returned, a dozen Italian workers were busy with picks and shovels along the carriage road. They were having little success. Despite all the rain, the road was packed hard. The work crew had only managed to break loose and pile up a thin strip of dirt across the center of the dam. The strip was not nearly high enough to hold back the rapidly rising waters.

Meanwhile, on the west side of the dam, more workmen were chipping away at a second spillway. They cleared out a two-foot trench, where the water quickly gushed through. Still, it hardly made any difference. At the original spillway, some men were working to unclog the weir screens. Branches, twigs, and other debris were making the main spillway useless. One worker suggested removing the screens and knocking down the spillway bridge to allow more water out of the lake. But Unger hesitated. He did not want to lose the club's prize fish. Eventually, though, he decided there was no other choice. At last, Unger decided the spillway screens had to go. But he had waited too long. Now, the weir was so entangled with branches and other debris, that it could not be budged.

The greatest danger to the dam was one not even visible to an untrained eye. The center had begun to sag slightly, maybe only a foot or two. The weakest point of an earthen dam is its center and should be the last spot water rushes over. At the South Fork Dam, the center was the lowest point along the breast, partly because the cast-iron sluice pipes and most of the stone culvert had been removed. The fact that Ruff had sliced off two feet of the height only made matters worse. The first place the South Fork Dam would overtop would be the center.

By 11:00, the water in Lake Conemaugh was nearly level with the top of the dam. Several serious leaks had punched through the exterior as well. Once the waters began overtopping the dam, the runoff would tear away at the exterior riprap. Attempts to save the dam had failed. Unger knew it was time to spread the word. People in the towns that dotted the valley below would have to prepare for the worst.

3 Three Warnings

There was a telephone line from the clubhouse to South Fork, but it was only in service during the summer. The line was not yet hooked up. So around 11:30, John Parke hurried on horseback to South Fork. Ten minutes later, his galloping horse was splashing down Railroad Street. He warned everyone on the street that the dam might go. The people of South Fork questioned Parke's news. Earlier, two men—well-respected in South Fork—had already come down from the dam and told everyone there was no danger of the water spilling over the top. But Parke insisted that someone must go to the railroad's telegraph tower and get a message to Johnstown.

The operator at the South Fork tower Friday morning was Miss Emma Ehrenfeld. All of a sudden, the man Parke sent came bursting into the tower. "Notify Johnstown right away about the dam," he said. "It's rising very fast, and there's danger of the reservoir breaking." Ehrenfeld was confused about whether or not to believe the man. Although she could not remember his name, she had seen him around South Fork. He was someone the townspeople did not trust. Ehrenfeld could not send the warning directly to Johnstown because the telegraph lines had been damaged by the storm. She had to send the message to the next tower, four miles down the river at Mineral Point. The operator there, W.H. Pickerell, had been working along the Little Conemaugh for 15 years. Ehrenfeld decided to "talk" the situation over with Pickerell. She tapped out the problem and waited for an answer. Pickerell told her that they should not take risks on the dam breaking. However, he continued to explain that, with wires down, he had no way of getting a message directly to Johnstown. He took the message and said he would send it on to East Conemaugh if someone happened to walk along the tracks below his tower. The two operators also sent a message to the yardmaster at Conemaugh and to the superintendent of the Pennsylvania Railroad, Robert Pitcairn, in Pittsburgh.

Before long, a trackman came by Pickerell's tower. He had been sent from East Conemaugh to flag a landslide at Buttermilk Falls, which was west of the tower. The trackman delivered the folded-up message to his foreman, L.L. Rusher, at Buttermilk Falls. Rusher told the trackman to head back to Mineral Point in case there were more messages, and he started for East Conemaugh. As it turned out, Rusher only had to go as far as a tower known as the "AO" tower, a mile and a half from Mineral Point and a little more than a mile upriver from East Conemaugh. To the west of AO tower, the lines were still clear. Immediately, the AO operator sent the message on to East Conemaugh and Johnstown. In Johnstown, Pennsylvania Railroad's freight agent, Frank Deckert, received the message sometime between noon and 1:00. It was the first of three warnings passed down the valley that day.

In Johnstown, agent Frank Deckert noticed a wire message had come in from South Fork. It was around noon when he picked it up. Like any other time the valley got pummeled with heavy rains, the wire warned that the dam might go. However, after countless warnings just like this one, the dam

(continues on page 36)

In Their Own Words:
Testimony of Miss Emma Ehrenfeld

In the investigations that followed the flood, telegraph operators along the Conemaugh River were called in to give testimony to the events that had happened that day. Below is
Emma Ehrenfeld's testimony, as recorded in *The 1889 Flood
in Johnstown, Pennsylvania*, by Michael McGough.

Q. *Miss Ehrenfeld, tell me where you were employed in May
last, and by whom.*

A. I was working at South Fork in the telegraph tower. I
went on duty at 7:00 in the morning. It was raining very
hard when I went down. I found orders there to hold all
trains east for orders. No. 20 was there, and I got order
for them, and they went on east to Sonman. There was
an A Extra, and I got orders for them also to go east.
The 1167 was on South Fork in the middle siding, and
the 1163 was just west of the tower on Argyle siding,
for orders. Limited came there at 8:46, ten minutes late.
They were there, I judge until between 1:30 and 1:45 [in
the afternoon] when they pulled over the bridge to the
station. The conductor came to me, and said he thought
it best to go to the station on account of the water, and
the danger of the bridge going out, and in case I got
orders for them, they would be there. Of course, that
was the last I saw of Limited, after they went to the station. Then, about noon, I judge it was, a man came in
very much excited; he says "Notify Johnstown right away

about the dam." He said, "It's rising very fast and there's danger of the reservoir breaking." I said, "Who told you all this?" And he said, "There's a man came down from the lake, and he told me." We didn't have any wires then. Our wires were all down, and I couldn't work with Johnstown direct."

Q. *Who was that person?*

A. I think his name was Wetzengreist, or something like that. I didn't know the man personally. He is a man that people generally don't have much confidence in, and for that reason, I scarcely knew what to do under the circumstances. Had it been a person I knew very well, or if he had given me a message, it would have been different. But he just told me this in a very excited manner, and I scarcely knew what to do. Of course, I knew the water was high in the river . . . so I called the operator and Mineral Point. He was the only one I could work with west. I told him, and we fixed up a message, and I asked him to send it. He said he could send it west from there with one of the division men. . . . I don't know how it was worded, but anyway, that there was danger at the reservoir. It was directed to the agent at Johnstown and the Yard Master at Conemaugh. [The trackman carried it] to the next office west, and they were to forward it to Conemaugh and Johnstown by wire. Whether it ever reached Johnstown, I am unable to say. About 1:30 or 1:45, the agent came and he gave me a message addressed to Mr. Pitcairn in Pittsburgh. I told him about the wires, and the only things I could do was to send it just as I did the other one.

(continued from page 33)
still stood. Why should this day be any different? He pushed
the message aside and went back to work.

Shortly after 1:00 that afternoon, J.P. Wilson, the superintendent of miners for the Argyle Coal Company at South
Fork, received more distressing news about the dam. Apparently, he had sent someone up to the dam to check on it.
Lake Conemaugh was spilling over the middle of the dam in
a 50- to 60-foot-wide glassy sheet and also on the west side.

The force of the water that rushed from that Lake Conemaugh
was so powerful it barreled through town and destroyed
everything in its path, only stopping when it reached a stone
bridge *(above)*. Messages warning Johnstown of possible dam
collapse were initially cast aside and were only taken seriously
after the dam had burst.

Wilson rushed a message to Emma Ehrenfeld at the South Fork telegraph tower. Ehrenfeld sent a second warning to Mineral Point. According to testimony by C.P. Dougherty, South Fork's agent for the Pennsylvania Railroad, in *The 1889 Flood in Johnstown, Pennsylvania*, the message read, "From all information we can get from South Fork Dam, it is running over at the west side and middle, and it is now becoming very dangerous." At Mineral Point, Pickerell received the message at 1:52. Once again, he sent the trackman down the tracks to the AO tower. And the second warning traveled on down to East Conemaugh and Johnstown.

Emma Ehrenfeld wired a final warning not even a half hour later. By this time, not only was water overtopping the dam, but it was also gushing out a gaping hole in the middle. The message read, "The dam is becoming dangerous and may possibly go." These words reached Mineral Point at 2:25. Miraculously, for a brief moment the circuit connected between Mineral Point and East Conemaugh. Perhaps the crippled wire lifted out of the Little Conemaugh River just in that crucial moment. The message was passed down to Frank Deckert in Johnstown.

Sometime between 2:45 and 3:00, Deckert got the third message. Finally, he decided to pass on the information. He called Hettie Ogle, who ran the central telephone switchboard and the Western Union office. At 3:15, she telephoned George Swank, the editor of the *Tribune* (Johnstown's local paper), who was keeping track of the day's events. Ogle informed Swank that Agent Deckert received a message about the South Fork Reservoir. The dam was getting worse by the minute, and there was danger of it breaking. Undoubtedly, the people of Johnstown could hardly imagine what kind of destruction a rolling body of water 3 miles long, up to a mile wide, and 60 feet deep could do to the Conemaugh Valley. But by 3:15, while Ogle was talking to Swank, Lake Conemaugh was already rumbling toward Johnstown.

4. Lake Conemaugh Unleashed

Stiff, cold sheets of rain continued to beat pitilessly against Lake Conemaugh. By 3:00, all work had long since stopped at the dam. Clusters of people just stood watching the draining waters eat away at the middle. The sheet of water spilling over the top now stretched at least 100 yards across. Concentrated in the center, the spillage cut through the dam wall like a knife. Finally, at 3:10, the whole South Fork Dam gave way, all at once.

Lake Conemaugh was unleashed to the valley below. The water seemed to leap out like a living creature—a roaring, ferocious monster. Thick, towering trees were snapped off or uprooted, one after another. Every bush, vine, tree, and blade of grass was scraped bare for 50 feet up the hillside. Later studies by civil engineers estimated that the water pouring into the valley that day was comparable to the velocity and depth of the Niagara River as it reaches Niagara Falls. In other words, the bursting of South Fork Dam was like releasing Niagara Falls into the valley for 30 minutes. Just below the dam, a farmer and his family escaped to higher ground as the waters rushed by, carrying their house down the river. It took between 35 and 45 minutes for the entire lake to empty. As it moved down the valley, it devoured everything in its path, leaving behind nothing but bare rock and mud. Located on a hillside, the town of South Fork escaped complete annihilation.

The tremendous wall of water gushed down the valley. Giant chunks of dam, fence posts, logs, and boulders bobbed in the tidal wave like toys. Up along the ridges of the dam, people watched in horror as the water ravaged the deep gorge below them. Just a few miles downstream, the valley made a sharp turn to the right and disappeared. Once the floods cleared the turn, all the bystanders could do was stand there in the pounding rain and imagine the terror taking place beyond the curve. With the dam gone, the road to South Fork

Like an enormous wave, the torrent of water released from the reservoir destroyed houses and buildings in its path and carried the debris in its wake. As the water flowed through the valley, some of the debris caught fire as survivors struggled to hang on to anything that would keep them afloat (above).

had disappeared. The only way back to the clubhouse was the long way—around what used to be the lake, through flooded woods and fields. Shortly after the dam broke, Colonel Unger collapsed. Now his work crew, with no one to give them orders, climbed down into the oozed acres of Lake Conemaugh. With baskets and cold, bare hands, they began scooping up the fish flopping around in the mud.

At the South Fork telegraph tower, Emma Ehrenfeld sat with her back toward the window chatting with H.M. Bennett, the engineer of the 1165 freight from Derry, and S.W. Keltz, the conductor. The two men had left Derry, a town halfway to Pittsburgh on the main line, Thursday evening. They had been up all night, delayed first at East Conemaugh until 5:00 Friday morning, and then held at South Fork since 8:00. Exhausted, rain-beaten trainmen had been in and out of the tower most of the day, inquiring about the tracks or simply warming up beside the coal stove on the first floor. According to the orders she had received, Miss Ehrenfeld held the Chicago Limited west of the bridge. After hearing all the buzz about the dam, though, the engineer grew uneasy about leaving his train standing right in the flood-water's path. Finally, the engineer stood up and announced that he was going to bring the Limited across, orders or no orders. Shortly before 3:00, the train pulled past the tower and depot about a half mile.

Around this time, Miss Ehrenfeld went downstairs to check on the stove. The engineer of the Limited had come back inside and was sitting comfortably, trying to dry off. Ehrenfeld talked with the engineer, then headed back upstairs to her desk, where Bennett and Keltz still sat. Through the rain-speckled window, Bennett could see the northeast corner of town behind the Pennsylvania tracks. Just beyond the tracks, Railroad Street turned into Lake Street, where the road headed uptown and curved out of sight toward the dam. Suddenly, Bennett noticed distant figures of people running for the hills. He jumped up from his chair. "Look at the people running," he exclaimed, as recorded by David McCullough in *The Johnstown Flood*. "What's wrong?"

Bennett mentioned something about the reservoir. Then, they all saw it coming—a rolling wall of water that spread across the full width of the valley. From where they were standing, it looked extremely close and enormous. "It just seemed like a mountain coming," Emma Ehrenfeld recalled. Conductor Keltz thought it looked about a hundred feet high, when actually it was probably only about 40 feet. The three of them dashed out of the tower and headed down the tracks to the stairs that led to the coal tipple. Ehrenfeld raced to the top and melted into the crowd of people running toward the back alleys that led to higher ground. Bennett and Keltz started with her, but suddenly remembered the fireman and brakeman asleep in the engine of their train on the other side of the river. They turned and headed for the bridge. Making it to the engine, they cut it loose, and with the little steam left, the train rolled back across the bridge directly toward the oncoming flood. Although it looked like a long shot, they had to try to make it to safe ground only a few hundred yards away where the tracks curved past the station.

The cascade was rolling at a rate of about 10 to 15 miles per hour but toting a mass of debris that included acres of trees, several bridges, mangled houses, dead animals, and hoards of other rubbish. Engineer Bennett's train escaped just about untouched. It had almost reached the station when another escaping freight blocked the way. All of the sudden, a heavy tree smashed into Bennett's locomotive and twisted it halfway off the track. With the water almost on top of them, Bennett, Keltz, and the two others jumped out and scrambled onto the other train just in the nick of time. The train pulled out of the way seconds before the flood tore past.

Located on a hillside, fortunately, South Fork suffered little damage. Beyond South Fork, however, the water raged

With the main line of the Pennsylvania Railroad running through Johnstown, trains that were in the middle of their journey were stuck in the mountains due to washed-out tracks and flooded towns. Like many of the houses and structures in the water's path, trains full of passengers were swept up in the giant wave that came down from Lake Conemaugh.

down the valley of the Little Conemaugh. From South Fork to Johnstown, it was 13 miles. Just outside of South Fork, the valley ran on an even line—without houses, only the railroad. The rushing waters shredded the railroad, ripped out tiles, and twisted the steel rails into crazy shapes. A mile downstream, the walls of the valley narrowed. The hillsides squeezed the mass of water into a wall 70 to 75 feet high. A mile and a half from South Fork, the river made a sharp turn south, traveling nearly two miles out of its way to form an oxbow that was only yards wide. At the end of the oxbow, the water crashed into its first major obstacle, a stone viaduct. The viaduct was a local landmark. It stood 70 feet high and bridged the river gap with a single 80-foot arch. When the tumbling tons of water and debris hit the bridge, it held for a moment. There was a horrible crunch as the debris nailed the stone and wedged in the arch. The water rocked back and forth, seething yellow foam. Within minutes, the water grew nearly 80 feet high. Then, it shot over the top of the bridge, gushing between boulders, twisted railroad cars, and broken trees. For a short time, Lake Conemaugh had reformed five-and-a-half miles downstream from its original location. Suddenly, this second dam collapsed. The water exploded, once again, into the valley with even more power.

Mineral Point stood just a mile beyond the bridge. The small town consisted of 30 houses set in a row on a single street—Front Street, which ran parallel to the river on the north side. W.H. Pickerell was sitting at the tower when he heard the roar of water. He looked up the track and saw a mass of trees carried on a wave of water. Quickly, he threw up the window and climbed out onto the tin roof to safety. Just then, he saw a man drift by on the roof of a house. The man shouted that Mineral Point had been swept away. Pickerell asked if the man knew anything about his family. From his spinning raft, the man yelled that he thought Pickerell's family had all been drowned. The drifting man managed to make it to safe ground, and Pickerell learned that his family was actually safe. Most of Mineral Point had fled to higher ground earlier and were now out of danger's way. Still, when the raging waters rushed through town, they gnawed the entire place right down to the bare rock.

At times, the growing debris would clog the entire path of the torrent. For a moment, the mountain of timber, stone, and chunks of town would bunch up into its own dam. Lake Conemaugh would reform behind tangled mess. Then, suddenly, the debris would explode again, as though it had been blasted with dynamite. The friction of the mass against the terrain caused the bottom to move more slowly than the top. Therefore, the top was constantly rolling over the bottom. As debris from the top smashed into the ground, a violent rush echoed down the valley. Anyone caught under the falling wall of water had no chance of surviving.

At Buttermilk Falls, work train Number Two out of East Conemaugh was stopped on the track near the hillside. Sitting inside the rain-soaked cab, engineer John Hess scratched his pork-chop whiskers, thinking about the rumors he had heard about the South Fork Dam. Farther down the track, workmen

The Reverend Henry L. Chapman was preparing a sermon when he noticed a B&O railcar floating in the floodwaters outside his church. The pastor gathered his family in the attic of his home near the large, stone church, one of the few buildings largely unaffected on the outside. The B&O passenger station in Johnstown, however, suffered extensive damage in the disaster *(above)*.

were busy with shovels repairing washed-out sections. After about 20 minutes, they heard a sound like thunder coming from up the valley. A few of the men straightened up, tilted their heads, and listened carefully. "It was like a hurricane through the wooded country," Hess later described in *The Johnstown Flood*. In the distance, the tops of trees between the railroad and the river were bending and bowing to the valley. One of the men shouted to the others to run. They dropped their tools and dashed down the tracks, searching for a place where they could climb out of the way. But the rocks nearby were too steep. They kept running for nearly 400 yards before they found a path to higher ground.

From the cab of work train Number Two, Hess still could see nothing. But he knew what had happened. "The lake's broke," he bellowed. Not knowing what else to do, he put on steam and tied down the whistle. With the floodwaters practically on top of him and the gravel cars clattering in front, he blazed down the valley toward East Conemaugh. The people of Conemaugh Valley understood the various blows of a train whistle. A steady horn meant the most urgent of warnings. Hess planned to keep right on going—through Conemaugh yards and clear to Johnstown—if the track was clear. However, it was not. He pulled the engine to a stop. With the whistle still screeching, Hess and his fireman, J.B. Plummer, jumped out of the cab in the nick of time. Not even two minutes after they made it to the hillside, the flood washed through. The whistle of Hess's engine had been blaring for maybe five minutes at most. Although not long, it was the only warning anyone in East Conemaugh would hear. Nearly everyone in town heard it and instantly knew what it meant. Many lives were saved there because of Hess's heroic actions.

FROM EAST CONEMAUGH TO WOODVALE

For passengers on board the eastbound cars of the Day Express, the five-hour delay in East Conemaugh had been dreary and long. They sat in their train cars, trying to find ways to pass the time in the dim afternoon light. Some passengers gathered in the aisles, chatting about the rising river, service on the Pennsylvania Railroad, or where they might get a hot meal. From time to time, someone would bring up the dam that stood farther up the mountain. But few were worried it would burst.

The trains already had been moved twice. Both times, the passengers had watched the river inch over the tracks where the train stood. Twice, the train cars had to be moved away from the river. Both times, the tracks disappeared under the water soon after the cars were moved. Now, the trains were on the last sidings next to town, as far away from the river as possible. The second section was on the track beside the depot, while the first section sat on the next track toward the river. On the other side of the first section, four tracks over, was the local mail train. The Day Express engines were about even with the depot, with Section Two a few cars ahead.

The last cars were next to the telegraph tower, the caboose of the mail train being the closest. In the caboose, train crews huddled around the stove to keep warm. The crew members took turns checking in at the tower for orders. Messages had been coming and going out of the tower steadily all day, including those from South Fork.

J.C. Walkinshaw, the yardmaster, was the man in charge of deciding which trains should go where. However, under the circumstances, he had little choice on what to do. He could not send the trains up the valley east because of the washouts at Buttermilk Falls and beyond. At the same time, he could not order them back to Johnstown because of washouts in that direction as well. Basically, all he could do was keep moving the trains back from the river. That part, he had done. Still, there was one more decision he could have made: to move the passengers out of the trains and to higher ground. Walkinshaw did not want to ask paying customers to venture out into the chilly wind and pelting rain and through a muddy little town that might not have enough shelter for everyone on board. So, even though he was aware of the trouble at Lake Conemaugh, Walkinshaw decided to avoid the headache of moving passengers.

Throughout the afternoon, Walkinshaw had been out checking equipment and watching the river. From 2:00 to 3:00, there seemed to be no change at all in the water level. He thought perhaps the worst was over. Then, around 3:15, the bridge below the telegraph tower let loose and dropped into the water. In the train cars, passengers gasped at the sight. Walkinshaw was not so impressed. Shortly after, his son

The powerful wave that surged from the broken dam smashed into everything that was in its way, taking with it the broken remains of homes, farms, and buildings. The muddy water churned the debris into fast-moving hazards that were more dangerous than the force of the wave itself. Few structures were left standing after the water came and went, leaving only remnants of a once prosperous town.

handed him another message about the dam. Like the other warnings, Walkinshaw shrugged off this one, too. At about 3:45, he decided to take a little nap.

Walkinshaw barely had sat down when he heard a whistle blowing. He jumped up and at once began hollering for people to get to higher ground. As he was running up the track, he saw the rear end of a work train backing around the curve. Oddly, the train came to a quick stop. Walkinshaw saw the engineer leap out of the cab and run for the hill. Just at that moment, the monstrous wave rolled around the curve, crashing back and forth against the mountainside. Walkinshaw turned and ran.

Inside the trains, people stood up and asked what was wrong when they heard the whistle blast. Outside the windows, a conductor raced between the trains, shouting, "Get to the hill! Get to the hill!" A few people bent down and gazed out the window. Their eyes widened when they saw the enormous wall of rubbish bearing down on them only 300 yards away. All at once, everyone clambered for the door. On Section One—the train parked between the mail train and Section Two—nearly every passenger got through the doors as fast as they could. Most people jumped down and ran. Several people, though, turned back to the train when they saw the mud and rain. An old minister and his wife, when they saw the flood coming, realized they could not outrun it. So they returned to their seats inside the train.

Once outside, passengers from Section One faced a serious problem. On the next track, standing between them and high ground, was Section Two. They had three choices: They could climb over Section Two; crawl under it; or run around the train, for four-car lengths down the track with the flood. Each person chose one of those routes. For those who ran down the track, around the back of the train lay another obstacle. Between them and the town and the streets that climbed to higher ground, a 10-foot-wide ditch gurgled with 5 feet of rushing, murky-brown water. Most people jumped across and made it to the other side. Others fell into the water, where they thrashed around with panic. Many of the people who had made it safely across stayed there to help others.

The flood wave followed the fleeing passengers into town, swallowing street after street. People darted in every direction. Some ducked inside doorways, trying to escape the rushing water. Houses toppled off their foundations and bobbed like toys. The sturdy, brick roundhouse had nine engines in it when the flood struck. Another 19 or 20 engines were scattered elsewhere in the yard. When the wave came down, it crushed the roundhouse as if it were made of paper. The passenger trains were whipped and swamped in an instant. Section One was ripped apart and tossed downstream. Amazingly, Section Two and the mail train both survived. Section Two was on a five-foot embankment, which probably helped it. After the torrent passed, its engine and tender and six cars were almost in the exact same place they had been since noon. While there was debris jammed all around the cars, the 16 people who had stayed on board were alive and safe. The mail train was also still intact, mostly because the telegraph tower had fallen onto the engine and pinned it there. But there was no one left on the train. All passengers and crew had gotten off and gotten onto the hill in time.

Thirty other locomotives, some weighing 80 tons, were flung all over. The floodwaters carried some of them as far as a mile before tossing them out. As the flood drained out of East Conemaugh, it carried several hundred freight cars, a dozen locomotives, numerous passenger cars, hundreds of houses, and many human corpses in its tidal wave. Next in line was the town of Woodvale, which had a population of about 1,000. Slightly larger than East Conemaugh, Woodvale was the pride of the Cambria Iron Company. The town essentially had been

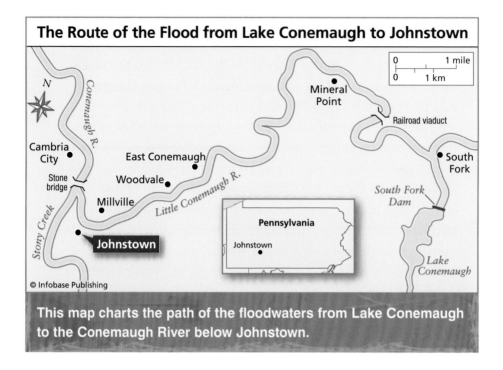

The Route of the Flood from Lake Conemaugh to Johnstown

This map charts the path of the floodwaters from Lake Conemaugh to the Conemaugh River below Johnstown.

built by the company, and it boasted streets of clean, white houses. A streetcar line that ran along Maple Avenue connected Woodvale to Johnstown.

Unlike East Conemaugh, Woodvale received no whistle warning. The wave dealt its destruction in a rushing blow that lasted all of five minutes. Only one building was left standing in town—the woolen mill, built by Cambria Iron. A slender fringe of houses on the foothills also remained. Otherwise, not a tree, telegraph pole, or railroad track marked any spot where Woodvale had stood. Two hundred and fifty-five houses had been washed away. That day, 314 people died in the flood at Woodvale, meaning 1 out of every 3 people in town had been killed.

As it continued, the flood broke up the wireworks, unleashing miles and miles of barbed wire into the mangled wreckage and water. Not quite an hour had passed since the dam opened up. The rain still riddled the valley but had lightened some. In Johnstown, just a few hundred yards from the wireworks, the water in the streets had started to recede. Though tired from the long day, some townspeople were actually able to cheer up a bit. It seemed as though the worst of the flood was over.

5 A Roar Like Thunder

When tumbling Lake Conemaugh and its mountain of carnage and debris reached Johnstown, it was 4:07 in the afternoon on May 31, 1889. The wall towered 36 feet high in the center and stretched a half-mile wide. From East Conemaugh to Johnstown, the valley opened up. On this straightaway to Stony Creek, the tidal wave began to gather speed. The force that hammered Johnstown was much harder than anywhere else on its 14-mile course from the dam.

Most people never saw the water coming. They heard it. Some described the sound as "a roar like thunder." The liquid avalanche brought with it hundreds of horrifying sounds—shouts and screams, ripping and crashing buildings, and shattering glass. Many people later said they saw something like black smoke leading the twirling debris. This dusty spray became known as the death mist.

Horace Rose had been playfully teasing the little neighbor girl, Bessie Fronheiser. From one of the downstairs windows, he dared her to swim through the flooded street and come over for a visit. There were only about five feet between their houses, so he set a piece of candy on the end of a broom and passed it over to her. Next, he passed a cup of coffee to Bessie's mother the same way. The lady was just raising the cup to her smiling lips when the first crash sounded.

Rose rushed to the third floor of his house. From the upstairs window, he could see nearly a mile up the valley. His eyes widened at the immense line of debris spanning from hillside to hillside. It gobbled up Gautier works, sending up a billowing belch of soot and steam. The mass was headed straight for Main Street and his house. Rose figured he had just a few minutes at most before they would be crushed to death.

On the corner of Jackson and Main, six-year-old Gertrude Quinn sat on the front porch, dangling her feet in the water. She watched some ducks as they weaved between the purple pansies rocking, like lily pads, in the yellow water. Her father suddenly appeared next to her and, grabbing her tiny hand, lifted her to her feet. He scolded her for disobeying his orders to stay inside and gave her a couple quick swats on the behind as he hurried her through the door. While the nurse changed Gertrude's clothes, her father, James Quinn, lectured her on obedience. He was smoking a cigar at the time and paused briefly from his speech to toss the ashes outside the front door. That was when he heard the grumbling wave and saw the dark mist coming up the street. He turned around and shouted, "Run for your lives. Follow me straight to the hill."

James grabbed Gertrude's sister Marie, who was sick with the measles, and darted out the door. "Follow me," he barked sternly. "Don't go back for anything." The Quinn family started down the street. The hill was only a hundred yards away. All they had to do was make it two short blocks to the end of Main, and they would be safe. Confident that everyone was behind him, James did not look back to make sure. He could feel the hands of two of his young daughters holding his elbows. But Gertrude's Aunt Abbie, with a baby in her arms,

Some people who were able to escape onto higher ground saw their houses and belongings destroyed in the water. After the flood waters left, people returned to the wreckage of their homes in an attempt to salvage anything of value *(above)*.

and Libby Hipp, a friend of the family who had Gertrude, had turned back. Aunt Abbie did not want to trudge around in the dirty water, so she had had second thoughts. Gertrude kicked and scratched at Libby to let her go. She wanted to be with her father, but Libby yanked her upstairs. Once inside, Gertrude peeked out the front window. It looked to her young eyes "like the Day of Judgment" she had seen in her Bible. Swarms of people were running and screaming, dragging their children behind them.

Meanwhile, James had reached dry land on the hill. When he turned around, he saw no signs of the rest of his family in the faces pushing past him. He grabbed the arm of a boy he knew and handed Marie to him. He told the boy to watch out for the other two girls as well, and then he started back for the house. He did not make it far, though. The wave was almost on top of him, demolishing everything in its path. He knew he would never make it back to the house. After a split second of thought, he turned for the hill and ran as fast as his legs could carry him. He just reached the hillside as the wave pounded by below. Looking behind him, he watched his newly built three-story red-brick Queen Anne house wobble back and forth, topple sideways, and sink into the mire.

The Hulbert House, Johnstown's finest hotel, was four stories high and made of brick. The hotel looked so sturdy that a local stonemason named J.L. Smith urged his family to stay there while he tended to their frame house. Astonishingly, Smith and his house survived the flood, but his wife and children were crushed when the Hulbert House collapsed into a pile of bricks *(above)*.

Gertrude never saw the wave. The crazed masses of people so terrified Libby that she yanked Gertrude away from the window. Then she dragged the child into an open cupboard. Aunt Abbie and Libby sobbed and prayed for mercy. Gertrude cried for her father. The broad house began to violently shudder. The walls around them began to crack. A second later, the floorboards burst apart and a flood of yellow water gushed up. Gertrude looked to her aunt, who was stiff with fear. The praying had stopped, replaced by the awful sounds of creaking boards and crashing brick. Abbie gasped and looked down, and that was the last Gertrude ever saw of her.

The next thing she knew, Gertrude was falling, reaching out for something to grab. She paddled hard to stay afloat and spit over and over again to keep the sticks, dirt, and sour water out of her mouth. Somehow, she crawled out of a hole in the house. It took all her strength to squeeze through. Within seconds, the whole house disappeared. Gertrude whirled along on top of a muddy mattress, screaming for help. She was weak and shivering—all her clothes except her underwear had been torn off in the torrent. Darkness began falling, and she was terrified.

A small, white house glided by, almost sliding on top of her. Gertrude called out to the man straddling the roof, but either he did not hear her or he ignored her. "You are a terrible man," she said as he floated away. After a little while, a long roof carrying perhaps 20 people sailed toward her. Again, she cried for help. One man started to get up, but the others tried to hold him back. He broke loose and plunged into the rapid current. His head popped up and then went under again. After going under several more times, he finally reached her raft and pulled himself on top. Gertrude flung her arms around his neck.

David McCullough recorded the story in *The Johnstown Flood*: On a hillside downstream, two men with long poles were leaning out the window of a small building. They were trying to rescue drifters as they sped past. As the mattress neared them, they stretched out their poles but could not reach out far enough. The man with Gertrude shouted out, "Do you think you can catch her?"

"We can try," they yelled back.

The man tossed her an amazing 10 to 15 feet from the rocking mattress raft. One of the men on the shore caught Gertrude and bundled her up in a blanket. The mattress carrying her hero continued with the current right through Cambria City, where he was pulled safely to shore.

For the people of Johnstown, the 10 minutes of devastation were the most desperate minutes of their lives. Men and women snatched up their children and hurried up the stairs to the attics

After the dam burst, Johnstown's Main Street quickly filled with water swirling with debris and survivors clinging to whatever flotsam they could find in the strong current. Some people were able to find safe haven in several buildings and roofs along Main Street, which faced a massive cleanup after the flood *(above)*.

of their homes. They crouched in corners as their houses quaked and crumbled. Once the wave hit, they struggled through the water, arms and legs flagging frantically. They grasped at anything passing by—roofs, doors, logs, and boards. Hundreds made it to the hillsides or sat on rooftops out of the flood's pathway. Unable to help their dying neighbors, they looked on in shock and horror. Washington Street, where Heiser's store stood, disappeared in a snap. Then, the wave spread out into three stretching tentacles. One path swept down the eastern end of town. Another wave rushed straight through the center of Johnstown. The third gush channeled to the Little Conemaugh along the north side.

Jackson and Clinton Streets, east of the park, turned into bubbling rivers of wreckage heading for Stony Creek. On Main and Locust Streets, heavy brick buildings such as the Hulbert House collapsed like cardboard boxes. Every tree in the park was ripped up at the roots and thrust into the churning water. Many large and sturdy buildings went down almost immediately, such as the Horace Rose house, the library, the telegraph office, the opera house, the German Lutheran Church, and the fire station.

The Hulbert House was the finest hotel in town. It may not have been as large as the Merchants' Hotel on Main Street, but it was newer. And it had been built with all the latest luxuries. Earlier that day, the four-story brick building looked to many as the safest place in town. On Friday afternoon, 60 people sought refuge inside its stone walls. Only nine of them got out alive. Oddly, just a few hours before the wave, guests had been discussing the possibility of the dam breaking. Like everyone else, they laughed at the thought. But at the first sound of the tumbling debris, they all knew that it had happened. Guests rushed panic-stricken from their rooms. Chambermaids ran screaming through the halls. They all stampeded to the stairs, climbing up and up. However, most of them were dragged back down as the walls peeled off around them.

Four minutes after the wave struck Johnstown, the water slammed into Westmont Hill, a cliff that rose almost straight up 550 feet behind Stony Creek. A vicious backwash swept up Stony Creek, annihilating miles of valley that had been well out of reach of the Little Conemaugh. Houses and rooftops carrying dozens of people spun off on the new current. Some people drifted for hours, but most floating debris piled up at the stone bridge. The bridge crossed the Conemaugh River downstream from "the Point"—where the Stony Creek and Little Conemaugh joined. Beyond the bridge dropped the Conemaugh Gap, the deepest river gorge between the Alleghenies and the Rockies. The Conemaugh Gap was the flood's only way out of the mountains. Luckily, the stone bridge was never hit with the full force of the wave. The bridge held.

Over the next several hours, debris quickly piled up between the massive stone arches—boulders, boxcars, collapsed houses, twisted rails, dead animals and people, and huge tangles of barbed wire—until it rose 15 feet taller than the top of the bridge. Eventually, the debris became its own dam, keeping the water from draining through. Johnstown became Lake Conemaugh, the waters standing 30 feet high in some areas. However, the raging waters would not be contained. The debris gave way, sucking hundreds of people under the bridge with its current. Still clinging to rooftops and poles, people who thought they had survived the blow suddenly were once again riding the fierce wave.

As the afternoon dimmed into evening, survivors packed into safe havens around town, most of them carried there on a rare but merciful current. On Main Street, Alma Hall housed 200 people. Dozens of people shivered in attics on Vine Street. Nearly 200 survivors stayed in the upper floors of Union School. More than 100 people crouched on the top of the Wolfe Building. At the Morell Institute, a training school for ironworkers, 175 people found cover from the rain. On the corner of Vine and Stony Creek streets, 90 people gathered at

When the debris in the water began to collect at the stone bridge in Johnstown, it slowed the current and created a temporary dam. This brief reprieve gave residents a chance to move to a safer location and to help injured or stranded people. Others who were not so lucky became trapped in the wreckage at the bridge and were found later during a search *(above)*.

the tall brick house of Dr. Swan, including Horace Rose—who had first seen the mass plowing down Main Street.

As the flood stormed Main Street, for a few minutes Rose stood hypnotized at his window, watching houses smashed like paper bags. The horrible noise paralyzed him. Then, he suddenly felt himself falling, and everything turned black. A moment later, he felt excruciating pressure, as if he were being crushed to death. The entire right side of his body had been pinned by falling timbers, dislocating his shoulder, breaking his collarbone, and cracking several of his ribs. He could hear his youngest son crying to him for help nearby, but he could not free himself. Suddenly, he saw his daughter's head bob up out of the water and instantly sink back under. Before long, a man seemed to shoot up out of the debris. Rose begged him to check on his wife and daughter, who both were still alive and had been rescued. Minutes later, Rose was reunited with his family—his wife, daughter, and two of his sons—on a single roof. They were carried by the shifting current to the Swan house.

In a period of 10 minutes, 2,200 men, women, and children were dead.

A BLAZE ON THE WATER

According to Reverend Dr. David Beale, pastor of the Presbyterian Church on Main Street, it was "a night of indescribable horrors." Wringing wet and filthy, shivering with cold and fear, Reverend Beale and dozens of other survivors paced the black shadows of Alma Hall. There was no food, no water, no blankets, no dry clothes, and no medical supplies. Broken, bloody, and often mangled, the injured moaned from every corner. The streets echoed with weeping, praying, and the shrieks of frightened children. All the while, the pelting rain continued. Though tired, they seldom slept. Their hearts quaked with each sudden scream and the howls of dogs and other animals. About 6:00, an orange glow flickered outside. Those who could

"They Are All Gone"

When reporters arrived in Johnstown, there were hundreds of heartrending stories to pen. One of the first such tragedies recorded was about Mrs. Anna Fenn, who lost her husband, John; all seven children; and her unborn baby. At the time of the flood, the ages of the children were as follows: John Fulton was 12, May Fleming Miller "Daisy" was 10, Genevieve was 9, George Washington was 8, Ann Richmond Virginia was 6; Bismarck Sullivan was 3, and Queen Ester was 16 months old on the day of the flood. The story, which is recorded in *The 1889 Flood in Johnstown, Pennsylvania*, first appeared in the June 3, 1889, edition of the *New York Times*, the *Chicago Tribune*, and countless other papers around the nation and the world. Mrs. Fenn said:

They are all gone. My husband and my seven dear little children have been swept down with the flood and I am left alone. We were driven by the raging flood into the garret [attic], but the waters followed us there. Inch by inch it kept rising until our heads were crushing against the roof. It was death to remain. So I raised a window and one by one placed my darlings on some driftwood, trusting to the Great Creator. As I liberated the last one, my sweet little boy, he looked at me and said: "Mamma, you always told me that the Lord would care for me; will he look after me now?" I saw him drift away with his loving face turned toward me, and with a prayer on my lips for his deliverance he passed from sight forever. The next moment the roof crashed in and I floated outside to be rescued fifteen hours later from the roof of a house in Kernville. If I could only find one of my darlings I could bow to the will of God. But they are all gone.

move crawled over to the window. They peered out at the strange sight of flames dancing on the water.

The drift at the stone bridge had caught fire in several places. No one knows exactly what started the blaze. Perhaps live coals spilled from a stove or perhaps a load of lime mixed with water and ignited a chemical reaction. Oil from derailed tank cars fueled the flames, which burned for three days. Many who had survived the flood, trapped in the debris at the stone bridge, would suffer a horrible new fate. As the wreckage blazed, it set off loud booms and claps. Men, women, and children screamed for help. After each crash, everything fell silent for a moment. Then the yells started up again. In the pitch-black, smoke-filled sky, there was little anyone could do to help. Survivors finally sat down on the ground and covered their ears, trying to muffle out the never-ending nightmare in Johnstown. Still, some people escaped the wind-whipped inferno. On hands and knees, they climbed out of windows and rubbish. These small, dark figures jumped from place to place, helping others. Perhaps as many as 500 to 600 people were trapped in the burning heap, but only 80 of them were killed.

Many brave survivors rushed in to help. In one case, a girl named Rose Clark had been trapped near one end of the bridge, half wedged under the water. Her leg and arm, both broken, were pinned down by logs. For several hours, a group of men worked to free her without success. The fire inched closer. For a moment, with the flames leaping around them, they talked about cutting off her leg rather than letting her burn to death. Just then, the leg pulled free, and they carried her to safety.

The burning debris cast an eerie glow over the devastated city. Nearly everyone was in some sort of agony. Some people wandered the hillside searching for loved ones. Others twisted in pain from their injuries. Still others collapsed in grief because they had lost everything they had in the world. Around town, people were still trapped under roof beams, unable to see outside or to escape. Others rode a bobbing rooftop through the night. Several people spent the night hanging in trees, the water lapping around below them. They refused to close their eyes, even for a minute, for fear that they might lose their grip and plunge into the cold, dark current.

Amid the tattered ruins of Johnstown, there was only one thing left for people to do: wait for morning.

6 The Survivors Emerge

Few people were able to sleep in Johnstown the night of the flood. War veterans commented that it was worse than any night they had ever lived through. Just before morning, though, a bizarre silence descended on the valley. People suddenly realized that the irritating, everyday noises of the steel town—the screech of mill whistles, the clatter of wagons, and the rumble of coal trains—had been snuffed out. How much they would have welcomed the racket that morning.

As the first haze of light peeked over the horizon, a few survivors emerged. Smoke and soot billowed out of the still-burning fires, and for miles around, the valley was blanketed in a gray film. Along the Frankstown Road on Green Hill, about 3,000 people slowly gathered. On the rim of Prospect Hill and the slopes above Kernville, Woodvale, and Cambria City, more survivors clustered. Some stood half-naked with the chill tickling their skin. Far below, a pocket of muck and rubble had replaced nearly all of Johnstown. A handful of buildings still stood—the Methodist Church and the B&O station, the schoolhouse on Adams Street, Alma Hall, and the Union Street School. The Iron Company's red-brick offices were still upright, as was Wood, Morrell & Company next door. Other than that, everything else seemed jostled and piled. The only familiar parts of the landscape were the two swollen rivers.

From Woodvale to the stone bridge, the path of destruction shouldered a quarter of a mile wide in places and at least two miles long. Between Locust Street and the Little Conemaugh, the land was an empty swath of mud, rock, and wreckage. It was hard for the people to imagine how it looked just 24 hours before, when saloons, stores, hotels, and houses pocked the landscape below. Across Stony Creek, Kernville had been mostly swept clean all the way to the raw earth. Below the

With the availability of coal, iron ore, wood, and water, Johnstown was the perfect location for Cambria Iron Works. The steel industry was a major contributor to the development of the town, and workers created communities in areas surrounding the mills, ironworks, and mines. When the flood thundered through the mountain valley, it destroyed the ironworks in Woodvale (above), a small neighborhood that was completely washed away.

stone bridge, the ironworks, though still present, had been shaken apart. The smokestacks had toppled over, and one of the biggest buildings had caved in. And Cambria City had been destroyed beyond recognition.

Slowly, the survivors down in the city could be seen stepping out across the debris. From the hills, the men started heading down into town. Closer to the devastation, the details of ruin came into sharp focus. Giant hunks of machinery, trees with bark whittled away, dead horses and parts of dead horses, and, most horrifying, countless human bodies were scattered about, poking up from an endless sea of rubble. George Gibbs, a reporter from the *Tribune*, wrote, "Hands of the dead stuck out of the ruins. Dead everywhere you went, their arms stretched above their heads . . . the last instinct of expiring humanity grasping at a straw." David McCullough recounted the horrid sight in *The Johnstown Flood*.

> People saw pieces of their lives littered around the town. Chairs, tables, toys, broken dishes, bicycle wheels, quilts, pots, and shreds of clothing were tossed carelessly into heaps 10, 20, even 30 feet high. Townspeople stared down a daunting task. Shoeless and bruised, many without a shirt on their backs, they started sifting through the mound, searching for some landmark or item that might show them where their house was. There were people, of course, who could not face the horror of Johnstown. They left, their homes and families broken. These battered loners walked and walked for miles, putting as many miles as they could between them and the flood. But most were determined to stay.

At once, rescue parties got to work helping marooned survivors down from rooftops and clearing away debris in search of life beneath. All around them, walls and wreckage still split and crumbled, and fires still simmered in places. At the stone bridge, more crews clawed at logs and jagged planks, hoping to dig out the living still trapped in the burning heap. Young Victor Heiser, who watched his home crushed, had made it to solid ground after a night in Kernville. He trudged down the west bank of Stony Creek until he reached the bridge. There, he joined rescuers, where they struggled for hours to free people. Without axes and other tools, rescue efforts were slow and frustrating. Rescuers could not save them all.

Many people scoured the town in search of family. They asked everyone they saw about husbands, wives, sons, and daughters—a five-year-old girl about "so high." The crying had diminished. Overcome with shock, people seemed unnaturally emotionless. At the same time, the tragedy brought the community closer together. People who hardly spoke to each other before the flood embraced like old pals. Suddenly, differences in religion, politics, and social status seemed unimportant. Survivors worked together, prayed together, and leaned on each other.

At this point, though, there was no order or organization to what was taking place in Johnstown. People were merely running on instinct. Moreover, the problems the town immediately faced were too enormous to tackle without a combined effort. By this time, no one had eaten in almost 24 hours. People were ravenous, and there was no food in sight. There was no safe water to drink. Thousands were homeless, and hundreds suffered, sick or injured, without dry clothing or medicine. Few people had any money, except perhaps some change in their pockets when the wave struck. Even so, the stores had nothing to sell. Every telegraph office and telephone line in the area had been leveled. Bridges were washed out or damaged and miles of railroad track were destroyed. It was obvious that the town needed a plan.

At 3:00 on Saturday afternoon, the townspeople called a meeting that became known as Johnstown's Citizens' Committee. Every able-bodied man crowded into the Adams

Street schoolhouse. Their first order of business was to elect a "mayor." They elected Arthur Moxham. He immediately took charge and organized committees to juggle the town's most serious problems and to create work crews. One committee set up emergency morgues at the schoolhouse and at a saloon while another established hospitals. There was a committee for collecting supplies and money. In time, these workers collected $6,000 in cash from trunks and bureau drawers. Seventy-five men were deputized police officers and charged with keeping order. Already, there had been some drunken brawls and looting, so people were needed to enforce the law. They cut stars out of tin cans picked out of the wreckage.

REBUILDING A TOWN

Meanwhile, word of the catastrophe already had reached the outside world. Oddly, a member of the South Fork Fishing and Hunting Club, Robert Pitcairn, was the first person to spread the news. On Friday, Pitcairn had been heading east to check on reported landslides, but his train only could get as far as Sang Hollow, a few miles below Johnstown. There, Pitcairn climbed up to the tower to find out what the trouble was all about. The operator told him the lines to the east had gone dead. They tried several times to reach Johnstown, but it was no use.

Pitcairn was about to head east and find the trouble himself. Out of the corner of his eye, he noticed some broken-up wood coming down the river. As it neared, the telegraph poles began to fall, and the tower started to wobble. Then, he saw a man riding down the river on some debris. He was moving fast. After him, more people started coming, hanging on to telegraph poles or parts of buildings. Pitcairn and others on the trains rushed out to try to rescue them.

At dusk, Pitcairn sent a message to the *Pittsburgh Commercial Gazette*. His statement made it clear that the dam at South Fork had failed, causing a disastrous flood at Johnstown. He

Robert Pitcairn (*above*) made his fortune in the railroad business and was a member of the South Fork Hunting and Fishing Club with his childhood friend, famed steel magnate Andrew Carnegie. Pitcairn was on a stalled train when the rush of water, full of flood victims, rumbled past. He was the first to notify authorities of the dam's failure and also contributed to the recovery and relief effort.

then headed back to Pittsburgh to help organize relief efforts. Pitcairn's first message reached Pittsburgh around 7:00 Friday evening. By the time he sent a more detailed statement from New Florence, the *Gazette* already had sent reporters to the scene of the disaster. At dawn on Saturday, June 1, a group of reporters stood among the people on the hillsides, staring in disbelief at the devastation below.

These reporters were the first of many to visit Johnstown. In addition, magazine editors, artists, authors, and at least 200 photographers also showed up on the scene. They described and photographed the catastrophe from every angle. Each reporter tried to outdo the next one's story. Oftentimes, their news reports were blurred, embellished, and exaggerated.

The newspaper accounts, whether fact or fiction, got the word out to the world. Across the country, people donated money and supplies to the relief effort in Johnstown. Within 24 hours of the flood, the first organized relief began at Pittsburgh, where Robert Pitcairn spoke to a crowd at Pittsburgh's Old City Hall. In closing, he said, as recorded in *The Johnstown Flood*, "Gentlemen, it is not tomorrow you want to act, but today; thousands of lives were lost in a moment, and the living need immediate help." As the people filed out, two men collected contributions. In 50 minutes, they had raised more than $48,000. By the time it was over, Pittsburgh would contribute $560,000, New York City another $516,000, Philadelphia $600,000, and Boston $150,000. Churches across the United States took up special collections. Schoolchildren sent in nickels and dimes. And 16 foreign countries sent contributions totaling $141,300.

In addition to money, people offered gifts of food and clothing. Cleveland sent 28 train-car loads of lumber. Minneapolis donated 16 carloads of flour. Cincinnati offered 20,000 pounds of ham. The prisoners of Pennsylvania's Western Penitentiary even baked 1,000 loaves of bread a day for Johnstown. Others donated coffins, blankets, nails, medicine, and other supplies. The world had responded to the Johnstown flood.

But on Saturday, June 1, the survivors did not yet know that help was on the way.

On Sunday, a train from Somerset came in on the B&O tracks around daybreak, bringing much needed machinery and supplies. Working day and night, crews replaced the great stone viaduct that had disappeared only a few days earlier so that trains from Pittsburgh could get to the town. Hundreds of volunteers, the militia, and state agencies went to work to prevent epidemics and relieve the suffering.

By Friday, June 7, 200 train-car loads of provisions had been sent from Pittsburgh. At the Pennsylvania depot in Johnstown and at the B&O depot, the platforms were stacked with cans of biscuits, boxes of candles, containers of cheese, lamps and matches, cases of soap, crates of canned goods, barrels of bacon, and hundreds of sacks of cornmeal. In addition, there were donated cots, mattresses, haircombs, pipes, pillows, teakettles, tents, cookstoves, and more than 7,000 pairs of shoes. Commissaries throughout the city had been set up, and food was distributed efficiently. Fears of a serious food shortage quickly fell by the wayside.

More and more workers arrived to help with cleanup and repairs. By the end of the week, nearly 7,000 men were at work in the valley. Enormous dining hall tents served hundreds of crewmen a hot meal. Servers ladled coffee out of buckets and passed out bread and a 10-pound slab of butter in fat dishpans. The eerie silence that plagued Johnstown on Saturday was gone by Thursday. Pounding hammers and the whine of nails being yanked out by crowbars rang across town. There were periodic booms of dynamite being used to break up the jam of debris at the bridge.

Perhaps the most impressive worker of all in Johnstown was a 67-year-old woman who stood just 5 feet tall—Clara Barton. From Washington, D.C., she brought with her the newly organized American Red Cross. Barton and her delegation of 50 doctors and nurses arrived early Wednesday morning,

Renowned for her dedication to the suffering, Clara Barton *(above)* stormed into Johnstown with a team of doctors and nurses and stayed for five months. Her efforts to help the victims of the flood became the first great mission of the American Red Cross.

and Barton did not leave Johnstown for five months. While they were there, the American Red Cross distributed $211,000 worth of new or used supplies. Known as the Angel of the Battlefield, Barton had been a nurse in the Civil War. In 1881, she established an American branch of the International Red Cross. She already had been on several missions: to Ohio during the floods of 1884, to Texas during the famine of 1887, to Illinois after a tornado in 1888, and, later that same year, to Florida during a yellow-fever epidemic.

Her past experiences, however, were nothing compared to the disaster at Johnstown. She realized this fact the moment she laid eyes on the valley from her train window. At once, she knew that her Red Cross had been faced with its first major disaster. She set up her headquarters inside an abandoned railroad car. Using a packing box as a desk, Barton began issuing orders. Hospital tents were set up immediately. Construction started on temporary "hotels" for the homeless. Also, she took a house-to-house survey to see how many people needed attention. She discovered that many people with serious injuries had been too weak or too depressed to get any help.

Barton and her workers did their best to tend to everyone they could. Barton worked around the clock, directing volunteers and distributing blankets, clothing, food, and cash. While in Johnstown, Barton lived like a local. She got what little sleep she could afford on a hard, narrow cot. She did not take nonsense from anyone. In fact, she spoke her mind to the head of the Philadelphia chapter of the Red Cross. After a few run-ins, the two groups would have nothing to do with each other.

Before long, the Red Cross's several large tents were operating the cleanest, most efficient hospitals in town. Six two-story hotels, equipped with hot and cold running water, kitchens, and laundries, had been built with some of the flood lumber. Barton lived in a command tent, topped with a whipping Red Cross banner. She was the most popular volunteer among the people of Johnstown and firmly proclaimed that the Red Cross would stay there as long as there was work to do. "We are always the last to leave the field," she said, as quoted in *The Johnstown Flood*.

While Barton coordinated the relief effort, the state was in charge of the massive cleanup. The governor of Pennsylvania feared for public health, not only for survivors of the flood, but also in the many other communities that got water from the Conemaugh. Sanitation was a major concern. Each day, the weather got warmer, speeding up decomposition of bodies and animal carcasses. The water that flowed beneath the debris

Tall Tales of Thieves and Thugs

The drama in Johnstown sparked the imaginations of many reporters looking for a colorful story. Quickly, they began spinning tales of Hungarian thieves who were supposedly stealing jewelry and trinkets off the bodies of dead flood victims. Some "news" stories described these "wild beasts" slicing off fingers for gold wedding bands, and one account even claimed a man had decapitated a woman to steal her necklace. Naturally, these stories also included a gallant hero who swooped down to recover the plunder and deal punishment to the appalling criminal. Below is an excerpt from the *Times* about one such fabricated incident. The words were later reprinted in Michael McGough's *The 1889 Flood in Johnstown, Pennsylvania*.

"With revolver leveled at the scoundrels the lead of the posse shouted: 'Throw up your hands or I'll blow your heads off.'"

"With blanched faces and trembling forms they obeyed and begged for mercy. They were searched, and as their pockets were emptied of the finds . . . a bloody finger of an infant encircled with two tiny gold rings was found among the plunder in their leader's pocket. A cry went up, 'Lynch them!' Without a moment's delay, ropes were thrown around their necks and they were dangling to the limbs of a tree, in the branches of which an hour before were entangled the bodies of a dead father and son. After an hour the ropes were cut and the bodies lowered and carried to a pile of rocks in the forest on the hill above."

Like this story, most of the accounts were completely fiction.

turned foul-smelling. The state Board of Health organized a sanitary corps to cremate animal carcasses, clean out clogged cellars, and disinfect. The Sanitary Corps was so effective that there was only one outbreak of disease. Between June 10 and July 25, 461 people became sick with typhoid fever. Forty of them died.

The heap of debris at the stone bridge presented the biggest challenge for cleanup crews. Finding something to move the more than 30 acres of tightly tangled, charred, soaked rubble was a tough task. The state called in a demolition expert from Pittsburgh named Arthur Kirk, also known as the Prince of Dynamiters. Using 1,000 pounds of explosives, Kirk began blasting on June 5. Even the Prince of Dynamiters had a hard

Because Cambria Iron Works needed a large supply of workers, immigrants from Eastern and Southern Europe flocked to the area and established communities in Cambria City. After World War I, however, foreign immigration lessened and African-Americans began working and settling in the area. Here, a group of African-Americans assist in recovery efforts after the great flood.

time breaking up the mass. By June 10, he had cleared only an area 100 feet by 300 feet. He decided to ramp up his firepower with a 450-pound charge, hoping to blast up the pile in one blow. Nine 50-pound boxes of dynamite were set at the base of the twisted mass, each about 30 feet apart. The entire valley and every building that still stood trembled in the blast.

For a moment, all work stopped around the city. The rumble was all too familiar to the people of Johnstown. They made it quite clear to Kirk that he should never pull a stunt like that again. Nevertheless, the blast had gouged a hole out of the wreckage. At last, a beam of daylight shot through under the arches. The blasting continued until the end of August, almost three months after the flood. Once again, the two mountain streams flowed freely through the arches and into the Conemaugh River.

The search for bodies continued for months. Even in October, bodies were found seven miles downstream. More than 100 morticians worked around the clock, cleaning and embalming the dead. The bodies then were laid out for people still searching for relatives. In the end, though, 967 bodies were never identified. Although counts vary, the most accurate number of deaths is 2,209. Of the dead, 396 were children 10 years old or younger. In the flood, 98 children lost both parents, 124 women lost their husbands, and 198 men lost their wives. Ninety-nine families were completely wiped out.

Despite their heartache and loss, the people of Johnstown dug into the overwhelming task of rebuilding their town and their lives. Soon, the city bustled with activity. By the end of June, temporary bridges had been built; the Wood, Morrell & Company store reopened and a few other stores welcomed customers; and the First National Bank was in business. In mid-July, the fires were lit at the Cambria Ironworks, and once again, the smokestacks puffed charcoal into the sky. Three newspapers were publishing by this time, too. By fall, temporary stores dotted the public square. Merchants could use these buildings for

18 months while they rebuilt permanent structures. The gas company had restored service in town by October, and by then, most homes and businesses had electricity.

The state militia withdrew in July, and most of the state cleanup work was completed by September. The commissaries, which had fed 30,000 people a day in June, closed on October 5. By the end of October, Clara Barton finally packed her bags. In closing, she said, as taken from *The Johnstown Flood of 1889* by Paula and Carl Degen, "Enterprising, industrious and hopeful, the new Johnstown, phoenix-like, rose from its ruins, more beautiful than the old." As she had promised, the Red Cross was the last relief group to leave Johnstown. Before Barton boarded her train on October 24, though, the people of Johnstown presented her with a gold pin and diamond locket—a glittering thank-you for all she had done.

7 Pointing Fingers

As death tolls and property losses climbed, the public grew increasingly bitter against the members of the South Fork Fishing and Hunting Club. Newspapers across the nation condemned the sportsmen and their lake playground. The people of Johnstown believed the club was responsible for the dam's failure and could have prevented the catastrophe. The members' carelessness and neglect had ripped lives away from thousands. Editor Swank spoke for all of Johnstown when he wrote, "We think we know what struck us, and it was not the hand of Providence [God]. Our misery is the work of man." His words were later reprinted in the Degens' *The Johnstown Flood of 1889*.

The countless coroners' reports that piled up ruled the deaths as "violence" related to the flood breaking the dam at South Fork Reservoir. Throughout the valley, blood boiled. Someone should be held accountable, they thought, maybe even charged with a crime. There was little doubt that the owners did not make the dam as safe and secure as it should have been, especially considering the many lives in jeopardy in the valley below. Ultimately, many felt the owners should be responsible for the great loss of life and property because of the flood.

This concept was not a new one, however. Back when Benjamin Ruff began establishing his South Fork club, Daniel J. Morrell, general manager of the Cambria Iron Company, was concerned. Few people feared the breaking dam more than Morrell. Materially, Morrell and the Cambria Iron Company had the most to lose. Although centered in Johnstown, Cambria Iron had numerous facilities and businesses scattered throughout the valley, including mines, forestlands, offices, stores, mills, and a railroad system. The industrial complex of the Cambria Iron Company alone was valued at $50 million.

When repair work was taking place at the dam, Ruff was unusually secretive about it. This behavior rose Morrell's suspicions. Because of his status, he was not used to being kept in the dark. He knew about almost everything that happened in the Conemaugh Valley. Morrell hotly disagreed with Ruff's shabby repairs and sent him several letters expressing his concerns. He also did his own investigations on the safety and stability of the dam. One letter of report, written by John Fulton, Cambria Iron Company's general mining engineer, is printed in this chapter. Wisely, Fulton held on to this letter, and it came in handy after the flood.

This letter came out in the open a little over a week after the flood hit Johnstown, in a sermon. On Sunday, June 9, the sun broke through the clouds for the first time since the flood. The sunlight warmed the air, and the hills popped with spring greens. The sounds of picks, axes, and hammers clanked throughout the city. Then, a new and strange sound joined the mix: church bells. Reverend David Beale held his first service since the flood.

At first, no more than 30 people gathered on the embankment near the depot. But as time passed, the crowd grew. Soldiers standing nearby meandered over. People came out from the depot, and others from the center of town slowly drifted in. Beale preached his sermon from on top of a packing box.

As the service drew to a close, John Fulton stood up and gave a speech that got the crowd stirring.

First, he declared that the Cambria shops would be rebuilt. "Johnstown is going to be rebuilt," he said, as written by David McCullough in *The Johnstown Flood*. "Amen!" several people answered. Then, Fulton began talking about another matter. "I hold in my possession today," he said, "my own report made years ago, in which I told these people [South Fork members], who desired to seclude themselves in the mountain, that their

When word of the devastation filtered out to Pittsburgh and New York City, relief workers and donations started to arrive in Johnstown. Residents and volunteers took on the enormous task of clearing wreckage and rebuilding the town while others began to spread the word about the South Fork Fishing and Hunting Club's culpability in the great flood.

dam was dangerous. I told them that the dam would break sometime and cause just such a disaster as this." A tense hush settled over the crowd. Fulton said what everyone had already been thinking. Someone was to blame for the flood, and Fulton had a piece of paper to prove it. All fingers were pointing in the direction of the South Fork Fishing and Hunting Club.

INVESTIGATION

In the immediate days following the flood, some members of the South Fork Fishing and Hunting Club outlandishly denied that the dam had even broken. One of these men was James McGregor, who was certain the whole thing was just a crazy rumor. "I am going up there to fish the latter part of this month . . . and I believe it is standing there the same as it ever was," he told the papers on Sunday, June 2. "Any other reports are simply wild notions." Unbelievably, he was not alone.

Then, on Monday, reporters from Johnstown reached the dam. They sent a series of reports from South Fork that ended once and for all any fantasies that the dam was still standing. Meanwhile, in Johnstown, bitter feelings already had started to fester in some people. After dark, an angry crowd of men marched up to the dam looking for any club members who might still be there. But everyone was gone. The mob broke into several cottages, smashing windows and furniture. Then, they strode to Unger's farm, hoping to find the colonel. Some people speculated that the mob was set on killing the club owner. Whether or not they would have, no one will ever know. By that time, Unger was on his way to Pittsburgh.

The club members who had been at the lake at the time the dam broke had headed off on horseback. Most of these men had no plans of ever coming back. Their quick retreat made things worse for the wealthy members. They abandoned the valley at a time when there was a need for strong men. If they had stayed and helped, perhaps the people of Johnstown would not have felt so much hatred toward them.

Following the disaster, a series of investigations took place to get to the root of who was to blame. Engineers determined that the actions at the South Fork Club had in fact weakened the dam. The investigation pinpointed four primary causes for its failure: Ruff lowering the height of the crest, the central sag in the crest that had never been repaired, the removal of the sluice pipes, and the blocking of the spillway with weir screens. Other individual investigations were conducted as well. In Cambria, jurors ruled on the death of flood victim Ellen Hite. The verdict was death by drowning, followed by "caused by the breaking of the South Fork dam."

Dozens of Johnstown survivors spoke out against the dam, telling out-of-town reporters what a menace it had been. They wove tales about how it had cast a shadow of dread on them every day of their lives. One exception, however, was Cyrus Elder—the only person in Johnstown to be a member of the South Fork Fishing and Hunting Club. He admitted that, while he believed the dam to be structurally sound, for years Johnstown people had been edgy about the dam. He had lost his wife and only daughter, his house, and almost everything he owned. But he took some of the responsibility himself as a Johnstown resident. "If anybody be to blame I suppose we ourselves are among them," he is quoted as saying in McCulloch's *The Johnstown Flood*, "for we have indeed been very careless in this most important matter and most of us have paid the penalty of our neglect." Naturally, his words were not popular in Johnstown, and few people accepted any blame.

Public opinions, coroners' reports, and investigations all pointed fingers at the club. However, none of the club members were ever held accountable for their crimes of neglect. In lawsuits, the defense attorneys argued that the water in Lake Conemaugh was coming up so fast on the afternoon of May 31 that eventually it would have spilled over the dam, no matter how tall it had been. If the dam had held past 3:10, it

(continues on page 86)

Danger in the Dam

A letter to Daniel Morrell, General Manager of the Cambria Iron Company in Johnstown, from John Fulton, General Mining Engineer, to report on the stability of the dam, November 26, 1880.

> SIR: As you instructed, I met a representative delegation of the [South Fork Fishing and Hunting Club] at the old reservoir dam fork of the Conemaugh River, two and a half miles southeast of South Fork Station, on the Pennsylvania Road.
>
> This delegation, consisting of Colonel Unger, C. A. Carpenter, Esq., Secretary of the Board of Directors, and a number of gentlemen, brought with them N. M. McDowell, Esq., C. E. [civil engineer], of Pittsburgh, to examine the dam in company with your engineer. . . .
>
> [The dam] was built mainly with rocks and faced with earth on its upper or pool slope, and covered with a riprap of stones. About the idle of the dam a cut stone arched culvert was constructed, in which a large discharge pipe was placed with connections with a wooden bulkhead. On the north end an ample overfall has been cut through the rock, seventy feet wide, to discharge surplus water during rainy seasons.
>
> After disuse of the reservoir, the wooden bulkhead was burned down and the dam neglected. The consequence was that the water, under its full pressure, with no repairs to the dam, found its way through the masonry of the culvert, and the result was the washing out of a triangular notch of the dam, two hundred feet wide at the top and forty feet deep. The resultant flood [of 1862] past South Fork and down the Conemaugh did some damage, the extent of which I have been unable to learn. The break occurred during a

time of low water in the streams, which very greatly modified its action.

During the past season the [South Fork Fishing and Hunting Club], which now owns this property, has put a force at work to repair the breach in the dam, so as to raise the water to its maximum height of sixty feet. The repair force began by placing large rocks in the breach, facing these with hemlock boughs and hay, and covering the whole with earth and shale. The facing of earth is being made with carts, the material dumped down a slope from the line of the top of the dam, thus gravitating the coarsest material to the lowest depths—just the opposite of the result demanded in this case.

It did not appear to me that this work was being done in a careful and substantial manner, or with the care demanded in a large structure of this kind. . . .

There appear to me two serious elements of danger in this dam: First, the want of a discharge pipe to reduce or take the water out of the dam for needed repairs. Second, the unsubstantial method of repair, leaving a large leak, which appears to be cutting the new embankment.

As the water cannot be lowered, the difficulty arises of [repairing] present destructive leaks. At present there is forty feet of water in the dam. When the full head of sixty feet is reached, it appears to me to be only a question of time until the former cutting is repeated. Should this break be made during a seasonal flood it is evident that considerable damage would ensue along the line of the Conemaugh. It is difficult to estimate how disastrous this flood would be. . . .

Source: McGough, Michael, R. *The 1889 Flood in Johnstown,*
Pennsylvania

(continues from page 83)

would have failed later. Even if there had been no sag in the center and the spillway had been working at full capacity, the same thing would have happened. Only, perhaps it would have occurred at night, when the outcome would have been far more disastrous. Unable to prove if a solid dam would have lasted, juries ruled the collapse an "act of God."

Perhaps there was not doubt that an "act of God" (the storm on the night of May 30–31) brought on the disaster. But to the Conemaugh Valley, there also was no question that mortal man was truly responsible. Human beings had made two crucial errors. First, they had tampered with the natural order of things. Moreover, they had done a poor job of it. Over the years, they had ravaged the mountain's protective timber, which in turn caused dangerous flash-flood runoff. The dam itself was the most dramatic violation of nature. A huge lake in the mountains looked bizarre for a reason—it was not natural. People in charge of the dam made matters worse by neglecting it.

Second, the people of Johnstown and the members of the club assumed that the people taking care of the dam were doing it properly. Sportsmen took for granted that the men who rebuilt the dam were experts. They never actually questioned these "experts." Furthermore, they lacked the common sense to know that a massive earthen dam without a way to control the water level was dangerous.

Many club members, perhaps out of guilt, contributed money and supplies to the relief effort. Some, however, never offered a penny. Andrew Carnegie possibly was the most generous, although he denied ever being a member of the club until a few years later when a member list with his name on it surfaced. The Carnegie Company gave $10,000, and he personally donated $5,000. Also, in September, he and his wife visited Johnstown to see the flood damage for themselves. Before they left, Carnegie agreed to build a new library where the old one had been.

In any case, the members' summer entertainment had been washed away. The fashionable cottages sat empty along the edges of a muddy lakebed. Boathouses, sailboats, and boardwalks disappeared. Naturally, membership declined and payments stopped. Finally, in July 1891, the grounds of the South Fork Fishing and Hunting Club were divided and sold at a sheriff's auction. Years later, the town of St. Michael was built on former Lake Conemaugh, between South Fork and the club cottages.

MOVING ON

The rebuilding of Johnstown stands as a vivid example of the human spirit's will to survive. Because of people's determination and dedication, the Conemaugh Valley rose back to life. Still, there were many who left after the flood. For hundreds, like Victor Heiser, the waters had carried away everything. If his mother and father had survived, he probably would have stayed in Johnstown to become a watchmaker. Instead, he abandoned the valley and worked his way through medical school. He spent most of his life as a public-health physician, fighting disease around the world. His best-selling book on his experiences, *An American Doctor's Odyssey*, saved as many as 2 million lives.

For years, people wondered how many of those names among the unfound dead were actually alive in some faraway place. Perhaps some men, in the first dim light of that dreadful June 1 morning, decided to quietly slip away and start a new life somewhere else. At least one man, by the name of Leroy Temple, did just that. Eleven years later, in the summer of 1900, Temple strolled into town and confessed that he had not died in the flood. Rather, he had escaped to Beverly, Massachusetts, where he had lived happily ever since.

Several fresh lives replaced the dead on that fateful night. Three babies were born, pinpoints of light in a city's darkest hour. They were named in remembrance of a tragedy and

The South Fork Fishing and Hunting Club *(above)* was empty when angry townspeople arrived to confront the members and owners of the resort about their neglect of the South Fork Dam. While some club members quickly left the area instead of helping with the recovery effort, others donated generously to help rebuild Johnstown. The club remains unoccupied and is part of a National Parks Service memorial site for the Johnstown Flood tragedy.

became the first symbols of how life moves on: Flood Raymond, Flood Rhodes, and Moses Williams.

It took several years before life returned to normal for the people of the Conemaugh Valley. Along the way, more faceless bodies were uncovered. The Pennsylvania Flood Relief Commission purchased 20,000 square feet for a burial plot high on top of a hill that overlooked the valley. Here, the dead would be safe from spring floods. The view was incredible—rolling hills of green that stretched off in every direction. A line of trees blocked the view back to Johnstown. Except for the grinding mills, there was no sign a city was even there. On May 31, 1892, exactly three years after the flood, the people of Johnstown dedicated Grandview Cemetery and the Monument to the Unknown Dead. The granite statue rose 21 feet above rows of 777 gleaming white marble headstones. (Extra grave markers were set in to make an even pattern.) Governor Robert Pattison was the key speaker. In *The Johnstown Flood of 1889*, Paula and Carl Degen recorded his words. He said, "We who have to do with the concentrated forces of nature, the powers of air, electricity, water, steam, by careful forethought must leave nothing undone for the preservation and protection of the lives of our brother men." A choir then sang "God Moves in Mysterious Ways" as the monument was unveiled.

After the dedication, the somber crowd, blotting tears from their cheeks, departed Grandview. The ceremony closed a tragic chapter in Johnstown history. Undoubtedly, some memories traveled back to a similar cemetery procession, on Memorial Day 1889, before the rains began to fall on Conemaugh Valley.

Chronology

1790s Johnstown founded by Joseph "Johns" Schantz.

1853 South Fork Dam completed, creating future Lake Conemaugh.

1862 South Fork Dam breaks a 200-foot-wide hole.

1889 **May 30:** Fierce storm begins in the Conemaugh Valley after dark.

May 31: By morning, Little Conemaugh and Stony Creek rise at rate of 18 to 24 inches per hour; at Lake Conemaugh, water level rises 1 inch every 10 minutes.

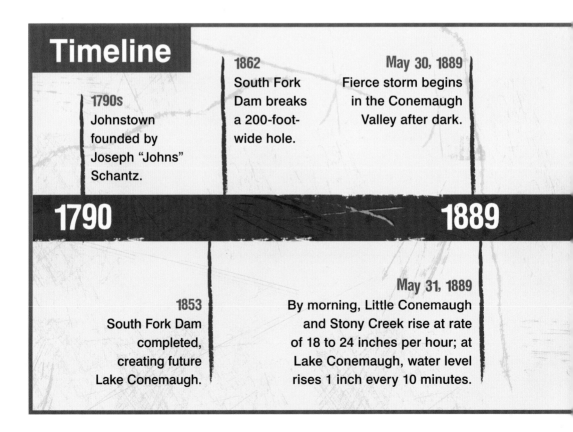

Timeline

1790s
Johnstown founded by Joseph "Johns" Schantz.

1862
South Fork Dam breaks a 200-foot-wide hole.

May 30, 1889
Fierce storm begins in the Conemaugh Valley after dark.

1790   **1889**

1853
South Fork Dam completed, creating future Lake Conemaugh.

May 31, 1889
By morning, Little Conemaugh and Stony Creek rise at rate of 18 to 24 inches per hour; at Lake Conemaugh, water level rises 1 inch every 10 minutes.

11:30: The first of three warnings is sent down the valley: The dam is dangerous and may break.

1:45: A second warning is sent down to Johnstown.

2:25: The third and final warning is sent down the valley; Agent Frank Deckert in Johnstown receives the message between 2:45 and 3:00 and finally decides to pass on the information.

3:10: South Fork Dam gives out.

4:07: Massive wall of water, 35 to 40 feet tall and rushing at 40 miles per hour, crashes through Johnstown; in 10 minutes, 2,200 people are dead.

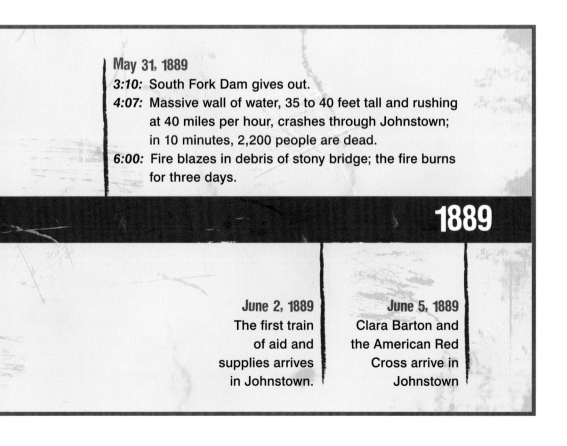

May 31, 1889
3:10: South Fork Dam gives out.
4:07: Massive wall of water, 35 to 40 feet tall and rushing at 40 miles per hour, crashes through Johnstown; in 10 minutes, 2,200 people are dead.
6:00: Fire blazes in debris of stony bridge; the fire burns for three days.

1889

June 2, 1889
The first train of aid and supplies arrives in Johnstown.

June 5, 1889
Clara Barton and the American Red Cross arrive in Johnstown

6:00: Fire blazes in debris of stony bridge; the fire burns for three days.

June 1: Survivors hold a meeting Saturday afternoon; they organize committees, work crews, and deputize a police force.

June 2: The first train of aid and supplies arrives in Johnstown.

June 5: Clara Barton and the American Red Cross arrive in Johnstown; Barton does not leave the city for five months; at the end of October, the Red Cross is the last relief group to leave Johnstown.

1892   **May 31:** The Monument to the Unknown Dead, to honor the unknown dead of the flood, is unveiled at Grandview Cemetery on a hillside outside of Johnstown.

Glossary

backcurrent   When the flow of a body of water hits an embankment and moves against its normal current.

freight car   A train car that carries some sort of freight.

morgue   A place where dead people are prepared for burial.

overtop   When the waters of a reservoir spill over the top of a dam.

pitch   The steepness of a rooftop.

recede   To decline or lower.

riprap   The outer layer of a dam.

trackman   A railroad worker who checks the tracks for damage and trouble spots.

weir   A low dam built across a stream or river.

Bibliography

Degen, Paula, and Carl Degen. *The Johnstown Flood of 1889: The Tragedy of the Conemaugh*. Fort Washington, PA: Eastern National, 1984.

McCullough, David. *The Johnstown Flood: The Incredible Story Behinds One of the Most Devastating "Natural" Disasters America Has Ever Known*. New York, NY: Simon & Schuster, 1968.

McGough, Dr. Michael R. *The 1889 Flood in Johnstown, Pennsylvania*. Gettysburg, PA: Thomas Publications, 2002.

Strayer, Harold H., and Irving L. London. *A Photographic Story of the 1889 Johnstown Flood*. Johnstown, PA: Weigel & Barber Printing, 1964.

The Johnstown Flood: A True Story in American History. Washington, D.C.: Guggenheim Productions, 1989.

WEB SITES

Johnstown Flood Museum
http://www.jaha.org/FloodMuseum/history.html

Encarta.com: Johnstown Flood of 1889
http://encarta.msn.com/sidebar_761593208/Johnstown_Flood_of_1889.html

Catskill Archive: History of the Johnstown Flood 1889
http://www.catskillarchive.com/rrextra/jfpage.html

Further Reading

Degen, Paula, and Carl Degen. *The Johnstown Flood of 1889: The Tragedy of the Conemaugh*. Fort Washington, PA: Eastern National, 1984.

McGough, Dr. Michael R. *The 1889 Flood in Johnstown, Pennsylvania*. Gettysburg, PA: Thomas Publications, 2002.

Strayer, Harold H., and Irving L. London. *A Photographic Story of the 1889 Johnstown Flood*. Johnstown, PA: Weigel & Barber Printing, 1964.

VIDEO

The Johnstown Flood: A True Story in American History. Washington, D.C.: Guggenheim Productions, 1989.

WEB SITES

American Red Cross: Flood and Flash Flood
http://www.redcross.org/services/prepare/0,1082,0_240_,00.html

American Red Cross Museum
http://www.redcross.org/museum/history

Johnstown Flood Museum
http://www.jaha.org/FloodMuseum/history.html

The South Fork Fishing and Hunting Club
http://www.nps.gov/archive/jofl/theclub.htm

Picture Credits

Page:

Index

About the Author

RACHEL A. KOESTLER-GRACK has written and edited nonfiction books since 1999. She has focused on historical topics, ranging from the Middle Ages to the colonial era to the civil rights movement. In addition, she has written numerous biographies on a variety of historical and contemporary figures. Koestler-Grack lives with her husband and daughter on a hobby farm near Glencoe, Minnesota.